D1461375

"Business transformation is daunting yet essential to staying relevant; urgency increases with rapidly changing customer preferences, aggressive competition, and unexpected world events. *TransformAble* is an easy-to-consume business transformation guide that will help anyone scale the mountains and avoid the deadly pitfalls of transformation. It is a guide you will pick up again and again."

—**MARCY KLEVORN**, board member, advisor, and former president, Mobility, Ford Motor Company

"Timely and timeless! As COVID-19 showed how quickly unexpected events can change our world, *TransformAble* delivers a clear, logical, and proven roadmap to successfully lead critical transformations for businesses large and small. This book is a must-read for your entire management team!"

—**JOHN BORIS**, former senior executive, GMAC and Ally Financial

"Captivating storytelling, entertaining illustrations, and totally relatable. Unlike other books, which often present organizational transformations in implausibly simplistic ways, Tuglus identifies realistic barriers, provides practical approaches, and gives you the courage to take on the challenge of transformation."

—**LESLEY MA**, CIO, NSF International, and former CIO, Cadillac

"Profound business transformation principles wrapped in a witty narrative. This book is an essential read for any professional looking to successfully undergo a business transformation or execute critical business pivots."

—**LEE SENDEROV**, chief marketing and digital officer, Foundation Partners Group

"This amazing and practical piece of work will open your eyes to what it takes to execute difficult transformations. It has helped me navigate complexity and avoid pitfalls at my own company as we rapidly build out a new billion-dollar business."

—**VAL GUI**, vice president, Upstart, and serial entrepreneur

"Always authentic and insightful, Tuglus helps business and nonprofit leaders alike light a path to a stronger future state and meaningful impact. This book is one I will visit again and again as we navigate new challenges and create new opportunities."

—**DEBORAH PARIZEK**, cofounder and executive director, Henry Ford Learning Institute

"Finally a book that takes on one of the business world's most intimidating and poorly understood topics. Real-world, hard-fought experiences bring to life lessons that would benefit anyone who is considering taking on a transformation."

—**TIM MCCABE**, former managing director, KPMG, and former CIO, Aptiv/Delphi

"*TransformAble* is a must-read for anyone involved in driving organizational change. Tuglus's insightful, thoughtful five laws distill this complex topic into an enjoyable and thought-provoking common-sense framework that any business leader can benefit from."

—**BEN SABLOFF**, founder and CEO of banking and analytics consultancy, AQN Strategies

"A pragmatic yet inspiring guide to business transformation across all areas of an enterprise. The conversational approach that Tuglus employs as she lays out the concepts of meaningful transformations makes this a fantastic book for all leaders."

—**JASON BRESSLER**, chief technology officer, United Wholesale Mortgage

"In a world rife with disruptive change, *TransformAble* is your guide through the vital journey of business transformation. Engaging and easy to read, I have shared this book with other executives, including all of my clients, and you will definitely want to do the same!"

—**PAMELA BURT**, business development executive, IBM

"Angie's insight and experience with business transformation is clear with this handy guidebook. It's a useful read and reference for any exec looking to transform their organization."

—**TOM TANG**, chief information officer, Alliant Energy

"Angie Tuglus has honed her approach to the complex challenge of business transformation. I've seen her go from delivering material business transformation in one company to driving change in many others. In *TransformAble*, she shares her proven approach with leaders worldwide to help make your transformation a reality."

— **DR. VICTORIA HUSTED MEDVEC**, president and CEO, Medvec & Associates, and professor, Kellogg School of Management, Northwestern University

ANGIE TUGLUS

TRANS FORM ABLE

How to Perform Death-defying Feats of **Business Transformation**

LifeTree
MEDIA

Cataloguing data available from Library and Archives Canada
ISBN 978-1-928055-83-9 (hardcover)
ISBN 978-1-928055-84-6 (EPUB)
ISBN 978-1-928055-85-3 (EPDF)

Editor: Jessica Easto
Cover design and interior design: Naomi MacDougall
All illustrations and author portrait: Angie Tuglus

Published by LifeTree Media,
an imprint of Wonderwell
www.wonderwell.press

Distributed in the US by Publishers Group West
and in Canada by Publishers Group Canada

Printed and bound in Canada

For anyone who is serious about transformation.
It's time to turn the *possible* into *reality.*

Contents

Introduction

YOU WAKE UP one morning to find yourself in an unfortunate situation. The world is hurtling toward you at a rapid pace, threatening to barrel past and leave you behind in the dust. You close your eyes and pretend it isn't happening. Strangely, that doesn't work this time. Before panicking, you try something else: you focus really hard, with all of your might, and try to freeze the world in place. Oddly enough, that also fails.

At this very moment, you, the hero of our story, experience an inescapably powerful flash of clarity. What has worked before is no longer working. Things are going to have to change around here. A transformation must occur.

Business transformation is not optional. The world is evolving at a dramatic pace, changing our lives faster than ever before. Rapid advancements in technology continuously make new things possible. Environmental catastrophes occur, generating cascading impacts through globally interconnected industries and economies. Lives become increasingly digital and connected. Consumer expectations change quickly. Meanwhile, ubiquitous access to information and heavy investment in innovation are leveling playing fields, industry by industry. As barriers to entry continue to lower, new competitors, products, and services are emerging and entering markets faster than ever. In every industry, established players are learning that once they achieve success with a highly profitable offering, maintaining dominance has become more difficult than ever before. An organization cannot sit back and live off a success for long, before serious threats emerge and force substantial business changes.

No organization, no matter how powerful, can stop the world from evolving. Consequently, as the world around us transforms, it is imperative that organizations and corporations transform as well.

Some organizations time their transformations with purpose. They carefully calculate the right time to execute, planning with regularity the implementation of advanced capabilities, to replace core operating platforms, aging product offerings, and inefficient organizational models. Successful consumer electronics companies are famous for planning out the obsolescence and replacement of critical high-volume, high-margin products this way.

Other organizations postpone their transformations for as long as possible, until the need becomes painfully obvious. Unavoidable. Until they are forced to mobilize. Until a retailer loses more customers than are gained. Until it becomes undeniable that a highly profitable product is now on the decline, with no revenue replacement in sight. Until a business fails to scale fast enough to effectively service a new product, losing their anticipated advantage over competitors, and revealing material operational and product delivery weaknesses. In some cases, an organization has waited too long and spirals into decline.

Triggering Events

Organizations often require a significant event to occur before they get serious about transformation. This trigger may come with some warning, as with a change in the regulatory environment. But sometimes there is little warning. A sudden crisis manifests that forces an organization to reevaluate and reinvent portions—or the entirety—of their business model.

The COVID-19 pandemic brought many examples to light. Education—from preschools to universities to on-the-job training to continuing education programs—is one of the most notable affected industries. The short-term actions were obvious: as people were instructed to stay at home and avoid social contact, many educators moved quickly to conduct classes via video conference. However, quickly following those immediate actions, a greater transformation had to be initiated. Every education organization was forced to rethink learning experiences, classroom logistics, and financial models. In many cases, they also had to address the other services that schools provide society, such as lunches for low-income students and supervision while parents and guardians are at work.

The triggering event may come through the arrival of a new leader at the organization. They initiate a material change in direction, introduce a new awareness of external forces, or spark sudden organizational awareness of just how far behind their operational capability is relative to their competition. In turn, this provides the impetus for a major business transformation.

These are not trivial undertakings. Business transformation is not for the faint of heart.

How do you know when you have a business transformation on your hands? It is when you are executing something of great significance, something that has never been done before at your company. When you envision a future state that necessitates a major paradigm shift in your organization: a new value proposition, a new way of thinking, a new way of doing. Reinventing your organization in the face of a crisis. Realizing your business model is no longer viable. Starting an entirely new division. Bringing an old company into the digital age. Restructuring. Replacing the core operating platform for a highly profitable business. Building a culture of innovation. Executing a bet-the-company initiative. Tackling a we're-so-far-behind-we-have-to-leap-forward-or-die situation.

Are you facing a unique journey that you have not taken before, without which your organization cannot thrive—or perhaps even survive? If you must urgently move your business forward in a meaningful way and the path ahead is fraught with peril, then you have a business transformation on your hands.

Business Transformation Is Perilous but Possible

In our rapidly evolving world, it is clear that business transformation has become a required component of corporate survival. Companies must transform in order to remain viable. And yet, when organizations finally work up the courage to tackle transformation, they fail at alarmingly high rates.

McKinsey & Company consistently cites 70 percent of large-scale transformations fail.[1] Programs run far over budget, and well past forecasted timelines. But not only that—critically, they often fail to deliver the intended business value. That failure rate, while intimidating, is only marginally relevant, because what really matters is making *your* particular transformation successful. So let's do that.

Transformation is hard. Complex. Scary. Fraught with political peril. But I can tell you from experience, it is absolutely possible. To succeed requires a mastery and honesty regarding the existing organizational ecosystem, as well as an understanding of how to transform it. It demands strong commitment, a belief in the possible, and no small amount of fearlessness. It requires taking ownership for your organization's very future.

I have spent over twenty years transforming businesses. Defining, designing, and leading transformations from concept to reality. The early years of my career were spent in tech start-ups, where I learned to fearlessly tackle challenges and always build with business value at the forefront. During my subsequent tenure at large corporations— including the multinational Ford Motor Company (ranked #4 on the Fortune 500 at the time), followed by General Motors Acceptance

---

[1] McKinsey & Company. "The 'How' of Transformation." Last updated May 9, 2016. https://www.mckinsey.com/industries/retail/our-insights/the-how-of-transformation.

Corporation and Ally Financial—I learned to apply this mindset inside large organizational ecosystems. It was there that I honed my approach for transforming high-level, visionary concepts into sustainable operating realities. I now advise companies across a range of industries and sizes, from start-ups to large corporations, including for-profit and nonprofit entities.

Disturbingly, the world appears no better at business transformation than it did twenty years ago. Business transformations failed at alarming rates then, and they fail at alarming rates now. Hundreds of billions of dollars are wasted each year across the world on failed transformations. That in itself is crazy, yet does not fully convey the true reality, borne by all those business goals that were never achieved. A failed transformation may impact corporate longevity immediately, or it may contribute to a gradual decline into obsolescence. The average corporate lifespan has been decreasing. According to the Innosight Corporate Longevity Forecast,[2] about half of the companies on the s&p 500 will no longer be there in just ten years. And Innosight forecasts this to decrease further. This means that you may be just one transformation away from rejuvenation or expiration. This book is going to skew the odds in your favor. If, that is, you are serious about transformation.

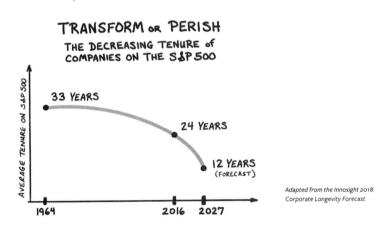

TRANSFORM or PERISH
THE DECREASING TENURE of
COMPANIES ON THE S&P 500

AVERAGE TENURE ON S&P 500

33 YEARS

24 YEARS

12 YEARS
(FORECAST)

Adapted from the Innosight 2018
Corporate Longevity Forecast

1964   2016 2027

---

[2] Innosight. "2018 Corporate Longevity Forecast: Creative Destruction is Accelerating." https://www.innosight.com/insight/creative-destruction.

All Successful Transformations Have a Common Core

Every transformation feels unique, but success relies on universally applicable know-how, one that is agnostic of industry or type of transformation. As such, the framework in this book applies to any type of transformation, in any industry, regardless of whether you seek to transform one part of your business or its entirety. It applies whether the changes are heavily technological, product focused, cultural, operational, or all of the above. It applies if you are in energy, food services, agriculture, manufacturing, consumer electronics, financial services, online or offline retail, or any other industry. In other words, no matter your organization's size, industry, or product offering, the core secrets of successful business transformation remain constant, and this is the guidebook.

Transformation is complex and poorly understood, but by the end of this book, you will understand it much better, and feel confident that it is possible. Whatever your flavor of transformation, this book will help you formulate and execute your transformation journey.

TRANSFORMATIONS BIG OR SMALL

Transformations look different, depending upon who you are and where you are standing. What seems small and simple to one organization may seem large and complex to another. One person may look upon the complexity of a $200 million transformation with the same trepidation another may feel upon contemplating a $2 million transformation. To a large multinational corporation operating in forty countries, the transformation of a single business function within a single country may seem small, posing little risk. However, in another company, one that only operates within a single country, this same transformation can be a matter of life or death.

I'm not going to judge the criticality of your transformation. Whether you are spending $2 million or $500 million, your transformation is high stakes for your organization. It will be a formidable undertaking, fraught with peril. To successfully initiate and navigate your journey, you will need to scale your timelines, team composition, and the seniority of your transformation leader appropriately, but the essential characteristics of your journey will be the same at any size. If it is a transformation to your organization, then treat it that way. Don't let anyone tell you differently.

One of the greatest challenges of transformation is that in the face of it, executives become paralyzed—even those who genuinely want to transform. They simply do not know how. Just getting to the starting line is daunting. *How do I begin? How do I know where we need to go? How do I hire the right leader?*

The journey itself can feel like driving a caravan of vehicles through a snowstorm or thick fog. *Are we sure we're heading to the right place? Do we know when to make that sharp turn? Is everyone still following, or did we lose some people? Are we driving in circles?*

And then, of course, there is making sure the business benefits are realized. *Are we preserving business value? Are we making the right trade-offs? As we arrive, is everyone prepared to take advantage of all the new potential?*

It feels overwhelming, doesn't it? It can be. However, when you step back—way back—and look at transformation from 30,000 feet, you can view it through a very simple paradigm. A transformation is about commitment and know-how, and above all, it is about people. At the core, transformations fail because people either do not know how to transform, or are not truly committed. Or both. Both know-how and commitment are absolutely essential. Being committed without knowing what to do will surely result in driving off a cliff and finding yourself deep in a common pitfall. Knowing how to transform will be equally ineffectual if you're lacking the commitment to support it.

Transformations fail because people either do not know what to do or are not truly committed. Or both.

At any given time during your transformation journey, there exists a level of know-how and a level of commitment. Healthy levels of both must be maintained throughout. How you conduct your transformation—the culture you establish, the type of leadership you provide, and the stories you tell—will greatly impact know-how and commitment. The combined strength of these two forces will dictate your success in conquering challenges, vaulting over pitfalls, and moving forward quickly to deliver business value. Is commitment high? Low? Does the organization know how to execute the current phase, and how to prepare for the next? When you're embarking upon a transformation, it is crucial to understand how to get the right transformation know-how and commitment—both initially and ongoing.

Illuminating the Path: The Framework

This book is for anyone who is serious about leading business transformation. It's for leaders who are responsible for enacting great change, who must turn the *idea* of transformation into *reality*, whether they are sponsoring the transformation or directly leading it.

I wrote this book because it is hard to find real, practical guidance on how to lead a transformation. As we know, transformations fail an alarming 70% of the time. Leaders like you do not need another detailed playbook, with endless lists and checkboxes. You definitely do not need another highly sanitized case study book (though they can be fun casual reading). And there are thousands of general leadership books with great advice, but they are rarely effectively targeted to this particular situation. Those books aren't cutting it. They do not get to the core of people, commitment, and know-how. This one does. Having experienced disastrous transformations—and delivered highly successful ones—I've gotten my hands dirty many times and can tell you what it really takes to pull off these complex, critical endeavors.

From initiation to locking in value, business transformation is a journey. A journey that involves diligent preparation, savvy scouting, and skilled execution. A journey that never looks the same each time. One that always entails a diverse set of new challenges, dangerous but entirely surmountable. Done well, it will ultimately position your organization not just to survive, but to thrive.

Throughout this book, I will guide you through the journey of business transformation, sharing the beliefs and methods that have made me successful. At each phase of the journey, we will delve into the highest impact, and often least understood, aspects of successful transformation. We will investigate ten perilous pitfalls and deftly avoid falling into them. By the time we have finished, you will be equipped to take your own transformation journey.

My transformation framework is organized into five phases, contained in five chapters. Within each phase, we will explore the most critical dynamics that must be understood, the actions that must be taken, and the epic tale that will emerge as you build and maintain

THE TUGLUS TRANSFORMATION FRAMEWORK

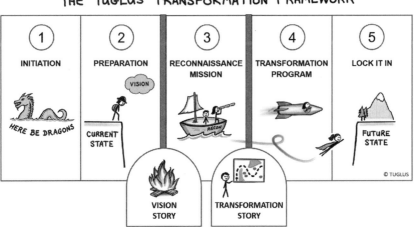

that vital know-how and commitment to lead your organization to achieve a powerful future.

The first phase, **Initiation**, will be an immersion in my laws of transformation: five foundational insights that convey the most critical dynamics of organizational and human behavior that must be understood in order to lead a successful transformation. Once you have had a chance to absorb these ideas, we will be ready for the second phase, **Preparation**.

Preparation equips you with everything necessary to prepare your organization to believe in the need to transform. Preparation also includes an overview of what a great transformation leader looks like. If you are sponsoring the transformation, this is the phase in which you will hire that leader. If you, yourself, are that leader, this section will help you identify your strengths and weaknesses relative to the role so that you can acquire additional support as needed.

It also includes the formula for a compelling **Vision Story** and the necessary steps to create it. The Vision Story, developed at the end of phase 2, is a critical juncture in your journey. It is the first of two evolutions of an epic tale that develops throughout your transformation. The Vision Story helps you build belief in the need to change among members of your organization. By the time we complete the Preparation phase, you will be able to confidently communicate, far and wide, the need to transform.

In phase 3, we will explore how to form and execute a **Reconnaissance Mission**, which will produce a mid-level definition of the future state of your organization and a roadmap to get there. This vital and often overlooked phase of the journey will clarify what the future looks like and demonstrate that it is attainable. This mission is a crucial activity to execute well, as it will dispel a lot of uncertainty. It will provide you with all the necessary information to develop a **Transformation Story**—the second evolution of your epic tale—a tale of the future that you can believe in and stand behind. The Transformation Story provides much-needed, tangible guidance for the Transformation Program itself, and it helps you secure commitment for transformation execution. It is a compelling tale that realistically conveys the future state, how the organization will get there, and what is required to do so.

Following the telling of the Transformation Story, we will be ready for phase 4, the **Transformation Program**. Here we will delve into the most integral aspects of Transformation Program leadership and execution. The program, while complex and arduous, is actually the best understood part of business transformation; however, there are still secrets and pitfalls here.

As the program ends, the journey is not over yet because the transformation is not quite cemented. That's why the fifth and final phase of the framework is **Lock It In**. Here we lock in the transformation to realize and sustain the intended business value.

During each phase of the journey, we will face perils. There will be dragons and pitfalls. **Dragons** are forces that impede progress and lurk everywhere, often disguised as other human beings. Most are not particularly stealthy and can be tackled directly. **Pitfalls**, however, are especially dangerous, and they appear exactly as you would imagine: sudden steep cliffs surrounding a deep pit, into which unwitting travelers tumble and become stuck. At a minimum, pitfalls sidetrack, slow progress, and distract travelers from the goal of building real business value. At their most dangerous, pitfalls are deadly missteps that destroy all of your carefully planned business value. The experience of tumbling into a pitfall may feel like an abrupt plunge from a great height, or an insidious, slow slide down to the bottom of the pit. Once there, you might not even realize you are in a pit. Victims feel increasingly frustrated about a lack of progress but do not know why. Or, sometimes, they may actually feel oddly comfortable down there.

It can take a long time to pull a team out of a pitfall. These excursions will cost you time and money. The greater risk, though, is the destruction of the transformation's business value and the cost of lost opportunities. While your team is stuck in a pit, the world continues to move by. Competitors emerge and improve themselves, and consumer expectations evolve. Instead of wasting time in the pit, you could be building new business value. The schematic below depicts the anatomy of a pitfall. Take a moment to study it. Note your team, sadly caught in a pit, while savvy competition flies past overhead and the rapidly changing world continues to move forward. This is not where you want to be.

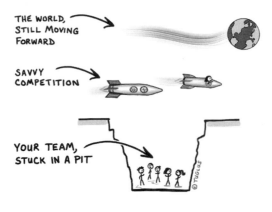

ANATOMY OF A PITFALL

Throughout our transformation journey, pitfall advisories appear at junctures where an organization is most likely to fall prey to a particular pitfall. As we approach, these advisories will notify you that danger is near. We will pause to identify them so that you may study them safely. This will prepare you to recognize them in your world, and to guide your organization safely across them during your transformation.

One last note before we head out on our adventure: At the very end of this book, there is a bonus chapter, **Search and Rescue**. This contains an assessment tool for when a transformation goes off the rails or becomes deeply mired in a seemingly inescapable pit. This special bonus section is especially targeted at CEOs, business sponsors, or leaders who must identify and deal with a failing business transformation. It is common to walk into a situation where a transformation is already in progress. Given high global failure rates, statistically speaking, there is a good chance it is not on the right path. If this sounds like your situation, don't skip to that section yet—in order to effectively utilize the Search and Rescue methodology, you must first understand what *should* happen, which the main body of this book will provide, before you can diagnose what is *actually* happening and decide how to respond.

Are you ready to do this? The world is changing so rapidly that your organization may have only one shot at this. So, let's make it a success. The odds may be against you, but this framework can help tilt them in your favor. You can do this. It is absolutely possible, I promise you. Transformation is a lot of hard work, but can also be an exciting adventure. Those interested in the adventure of driving real change, move forward. If you are not serious, this is not the book for you. Exit at any time.

What's that, you say? You're in? Excellent. Let's have some fun.

First stop, Initiation.

HERE BE DRAGONS

1
Initiation
Understanding the Laws of the Land

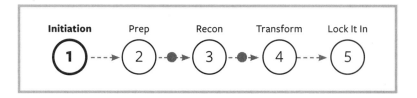

Initiation	Prep	Recon	Transform	Lock It In
1	2	3	4	5

WHEN EMBARKING UPON an unfamiliar journey, we can dramatically increase our chances of success by first educating ourselves on the laws of the land. Such laws convey the most critical dynamics of an ecosystem and terrain—and reveal how to best interact with it—in order to quickly and safely achieve our intended goals.

Recently, I spent some time hiking in Alaska. An excursion there involves wild animals, deep forests, ice fields, and glaciers. It is a land of many perils. While hiking, you might stumble upon a moose, a generally peaceful animal with poor eyesight that weighs a thousand pounds and could stomp you to death if provoked. Upon discovering a moose with a calf frolicking nearby, although tempted to get closer, I knew it was safer to keep my distance and made sure I never got between the two animals. I applied the same logic later, when a bear cub ambled onto the path in front of me—though I'll admit to a brief moment of terror as I desperately scanned the forest for its much larger parent.

Before traveling, I had equipped myself with an understanding of the dynamics of the ecosystem that were most likely to impact my journey, so was thus prepared for the most common and dangerous challenges. I successfully navigated perils, avoiding being plunged into a crevasse, stomped on by a moose, or mauled by a bear. Successfully navigating any dangerous journey requires the proper initiation, and business transformation is no exception. There are many things that can impede, injure, or kill you during a journey in Alaska. Likewise, there are many things that can impede, injure, or kill the value of your business transformation. Your business journey must navigate numerous dragons and pitfalls in order to emerge victorious over fast-moving competition and the ever-changing world.

This chapter initiates you in the laws of transformation: the core dynamics of people and leadership that are most relevant and critical to the journey of business transformation. These five foundational laws will serve you well through all phases of your journey. You will find them widely applicable to leadership in general, but they are *especially* important for business transformation.

Successful transformation leadership is not about memorizing a list of activities to undertake, such as risk management, project planning, change control, and budgeting. It is about understanding the organizational system that you are changing and its dynamics; understanding the people within it and what drives them; knowing where you are taking them; and being skilled enough to maximize the business value of the entire endeavor.

In Alaska, it would have been only marginally helpful to memorize a list of threats—moose, bear, poisonous plants, crevasses. And it would have been overwhelming and time-consuming to research each possible peril in depth in an attempt to absorb all the details. What was truly important was to understand the core dynamics most relevant to the particular journey I was taking—for example, that animals can become dangerous when protecting their young, and how that could impact my journey. Understanding the core behaviors of the system not only aids in avoiding dangers, but also gives you the ability to think for yourself, enabling you to solve dangerous situations when they do emerge.

Accordingly, my transformation laws are designed to convey the underlying laws of the land of transformation, providing critical insights into organizational behavior and transformation leadership. These laws have emerged from my over twenty years of transformation experience. Taken to heart, they will give you a powerful advantage. As we explore them, do not try to memorize them precisely. Instead, strive to understand the core dynamics within them. There will be no multiple-choice test, I promise. Let's take a look at my Laws of Transformation:

- It's all **people systems**

- People **fear** the **unknown**

- **Relativity** reduces fear

- You need **speed**

- You are writing an **epic tale**

1 It's all PEOPLE SYSTEMS
2 People FEAR the UNKNOWN
3 RELATIVITY reduces fear
4 You need SPEED
5 You are writing an EPIC TALE

Tuglus Transformation Law #1: It's All People Systems

I love getting to the core of something. Pulling it apart to see how it works. Identifying its central truths. Exploring the components and discovering the few, simple, underlying rules that make the system operate. Over the course of many years, I have taken apart almost every appliance in my home to see how it works. (I wait until they are broken. Honest.)

Similarly, getting to the heart of an organization can be invigorating. Like household appliances, organizations are also systems. But instead of gears and motors and wires and microchips, organizations are systems of people. And people systems are far more complex and interesting than mechanical systems. Which makes them a lot more fun.

You may never need to know how your microwave or furnace works. However, if you are embarking upon a transformation, you *do* need to understand the core dynamics of the system of people that you are transforming. Your very success depends upon it. People systems are at the heart of any transformation. Successful transformations take people on a journey, drawing on their sense of purpose, framing the future, dispelling unknowns, and building ownership in order to deliver real business value. Your success in instituting real change is directly proportional to how well you learn and master the system of people that you are transforming.

As you take your transformation journey—as you envision it and execute it—it is easy to become fixated on the seemingly more tangible aspects of the transformation. A cool new product with great market potential. Or an advanced technology platform. But I don't care how great your technology solution will be, or what wonderful feat of engineering has been designed, or how amazing that product *could* be. If the system of people surrounding it—the employees and leaders—do not take ownership for achievement of the vision, and incorporate it to drive business value, then your entire journey will be meaningless. Choosing appropriate tools and solutions is important, but that is the easy part. The real challenge is all about people. And systems of people are complex. In any size. This is the first law of transformation because it underlies all others. Everything ahead will build upon this foundation.

DELVING INTO THE DYNAMICS: OWNERSHIP IS LOST AS ORGANIZATIONS GROW LARGER AND OLDER

In a ten-person company, the motivations and engagement of people are fairly obvious. It is easy to mobilize and make things happen. There is not much of a people system to figure out, and it is easy to engage the entire company to focus on big-picture business goals. This is one reason early stage start-ups are so invigorating.

As companies grow, separate functions form—marketing, engineering, editorial, communications—and accordingly, the feeling of ownership that people once felt for the entirety of the company now splits as well. Many new employees join, and they do not possess the same perspective, the same sense of ownership as the original employees. The result is that with every growth spurt, every influx of new people, the original sense of ownership erodes. Natural attrition of staff increases this effect as additional new people come on board. The larger the company grows, and the longer it lives, the less the average employee truly understands and cares about the big picture. The less ownership each one has. Figuring out how to lead those now disparate groups of people, and guide them to band together for the common good, is one of the core challenges of organizational leadership. And this challenge becomes magnified and amplified during times of transformation.

UNCOVERING THE MYSTERIES OF HUMAN BEHAVIOR

It was in a company of 200 people where I began to recognize the complexity of transforming people systems. It is challenging to get a system of people to collaborate effectively toward a common goal. Figuring out how to do this was not always fun for me. Initially, in fact, it was quite frustrating.

Recently, I found a picture I drew back then to demonstrate one of my frustrations. The "risk cauldron" was a concept I created to humorously describe some of the dysfunction I was experiencing. This drawing appeared on my whiteboard quite often, whenever I was discussing a particular challenge with colleagues. Every time we got close to making progress on key decisions on our project, there were two people who would stir the risk cauldron and bring up new "very concerning risks." Frequently this would stop progress in its tracks. I was convinced that somewhere there was a secret cauldron of risks, from which they would pull whatever random risk bubbled to the top that day, and offer it up in the name of risk management.

This company was a small custom software shop with no official risk function. It was every person's job to deliver the solution the client hired us to create, and risk management was an inherent part of solution delivery. Neither of the people stirring the cauldron had the official job to just attend meetings and raise risks all day long. Even when you have a formal corporate risk function, this unproductive passive-aggressive behavior should not occur. But let's leave a deeper discussion of corporate risk for another day. Regarding that, for now,

MEANWHILE, DEEP IN THE RISK DEPARTMENT...

all I can say is watch carefully. If you see your risk professionals (or anyone, for that matter) tossing out seemingly random risks at inopportune times, check the depths of their department for a locked heatproof room . . .

Back to the story. It was not anyone's job to bring up risks and then sit back and watch as meetings were derailed and progress hampered. So why were they doing this? I speculated that their goal was to avoid doing work by postponing status discussions. Or to look engaged as a substitute for work. Alternatively, they were evil masterminds who were doing both, appearing engaged by bringing up "risks" at strategic moments, in order to derail productive discussion and ultimately allow them to avoid real assignments. That was my leading hypothesis.

I had many hypotheses. However, they only went a layer or two deep. And they remained only hypotheses. At first, I did not dig far enough to really get into the intricacy of the people system, into the interconnections of influence and motivation in play, to truly figure out why they were doing this. I was just so amazed and frustrated by how the behavior of just one or two people could dramatically alter the productivity of a larger group. Publicly and directly challenging the risk cauldron stirrers, as a junior employee, just caused them to double down on their strategy and suggest that I didn't know what I was talking about. So that didn't work. For a while, I just let it annoy me. But it was so puzzling. Then I began to ask why. I started to look deeper, to investigate. To peel back the layers of behavior to see what was driving this. What was really going on, beneath the surface, when this situation occurred?

From this new perspective, I began to see a system at work. There were forces behind the behavior. Through individual conversations with the cauldron stirrers and others, connections emerged. Most notable was the discovery of a notorious project in recent past where the client had been unpleasantly surprised by a very visible issue in the product delivered to them. It was widely believed that the risk of this issue occurring could and should have been identified and prevented before product launch.

Upon learning this, I understood why some people might be overly sensitive to risks. It also became clear, however, that one of the cauldron stirrers was indeed taking advantage of this situation as I had originally hypothesized. In an act of self-promotion, they were liberally noting possible risks, unproductively, in an attempt to demonstrate how diligent and engaged they were. And others were allowing it due to the lingering shadow of that recent event.

These were not evil masterminds. They were part of a system. A system that could be investigated and understood.

It was a few years later, at Ford Motor Company, where I really learned about people systems. There is no better place to learn about people systems than a hundred-year-old global Fortune 10 company. The only place that could be better is the government. Which I also experienced, as a contractor on a large program at the US Centers for Disease Control and Prevention (CDC)—but more on that later.

At Ford, I discovered that people systems are far more complex and interesting than physical systems. Earlier I mentioned taking apart household appliances. Have you ever taken apart one of yours? Open one up sometime. I'm serious. Pick one. Refrigerator, washing machine, furnace, microwave—no need to take it entirely apart, just unscrew the casing and peek inside. It will immediately become clear to you that there are very few parts in there. These devices are truly not that complicated. They have a straightforward system of connected components, and a limited number of failure points. Most often, mechanical and electrical components either perform their function or do not. Occasionally, they degrade and partially perform their function. But it is a simple system. Press start on a machine, and it follows the directions that were coded into it until a component fails.

Now people systems, those are complex. And fascinating. It may not be immediately obvious how a single person can consistently destroy the productivity of a large project, but if you put in some thought and effort, you can figure it out. It is diagnosable. And, it turns out, like mechanical systems, people systems are also solvable. They are just a bit more mysterious. Somewhat unpredictable under pressure. And solving them requires far more courage and consideration.

If you press start on a people system, consistent behavior is not assured. No matter how well job functions have been detailed in operating manuals and policies. Upon receiving the cue to perform their role, any given person in a business process may respond in myriad ways, only one of which is following the directions "as programmed."

For instance, they might perform a task differently because they found a better or faster way to do it. This alternative method might be truly better, or it might be a shortcut that unbeknownst to them creates more work for someone downstream. A new employee could perform a task incorrectly due to an unwarranted belief that they already know how to do it based on a prior role. Or because they asked someone else to temporarily step in for them, someone who does not know how to complete the task correctly. Distractions can occur. A competing request comes in. A coworker drops by to ask a question, or invite them to lunch. A friend sends a link to cute cat videos. Their focus shifts to that distraction and leaves their current activity only partially complete, or with an error. There are many, many scenarios under which the task may not be completed as designed. At any given time, every person involved in a process may choose an alternative path instead of promptly performing their role as instructed.

We have all experienced these situations. People are not finite, independent elements that can be set into place to automatically perform a function with perfect consistency. People are complex entities that exist within interconnected systems. It is difficult enough to drive desired behavior with well-documented, repeatable processes, let alone roles where the tasks are not well documented and the variation far greater. And during a time of business transformation, the stakes are higher and the importance is amplified.

UNDERSTAND PEOPLE AND ENGAGE THEM IN YOUR JOURNEY

When you're leading or sponsoring a transformation, your job is all about architecting an ecosystem of people to achieve a future state vision. Regardless of the type of transformation at hand, every transformation at its core is about getting people to operate in new models, use different processes, and behave with new mindsets and beliefs.

To succeed at transformation, you must take people on a journey. They need to know where they are going, and how they will get there. They need to know why they should care. And they must build ownership for the new solutions, the new processes, the new products and operations. Your actions along the way must take into account these needs and the systemic nature of your organization. Choosing not to understand the people system, while imposing change upon them, will not end well. Poorly thought-out actions can trigger counterproductive behavior, regardless of intention. Without understanding the system, you are likely to unintentionally power resistance and build strong movements counter to the goals of the transformation.

In contrast, well-thought-out, people-savvy actions will reinforce themselves, and we want to create this effect as much as possible. An employee who discovers a more efficient way to execute a process, and is then encouraged to share it, may inspire others to seek out and share improvements themselves. In a transformation, we must be ready to not only anticipate these things but also use this knowledge to make thoughtful moves.

Understanding people systems is everyone's job on the Transformation team. Program managers who do not possess a mindset geared toward people systems must be replaced. There are many excellent project managers who can apply project fundamentals to small individual projects quite well—tracking tasks, facilitating status meetings, adjusting timelines—but cannot make the transition to the greater people complexity inherent in transformations. They are not attuned to human behavior and are unable to anticipate it. They are unable to consider, or are unaware of, the differing incentives and mental models. I have certainly replaced people over the course of my career who just couldn't make the transition to think and act in terms of people systems.

Those people stirring the risk cauldron? There was something motivating that behavior. And there was something in that system that allowed it to recur. Often, multiple forces are at play, generating passive-aggressive behavior and allowing it to consistently impede progress. Understanding this entire system of behavior and action, while always a great skill for leaders to cultivate, becomes critical when leading a transformation. In order to lead, influence, and drive people in the direction we want them to go, at the speed we need, it is imperative to learn why such behavior is happening and how it is influenced.

Are you tired of talking about people? There is no escape if you are serious about transformation. People are at the core of any transformation. Knowing that, and acting with that in mind, is foundational to a successful transformation. The dragons stirring the risk cauldron are not the only dragons out there. Over time you will recognize more and more of them. Some will lead you into pitfalls, some will actively campaign against you, and some will be deviously difficult to recognize. And all of them can be understood through the people system. In the next law, we will delve into one of the most challenging aspects of the people system: fear of the unknown.

Success in instituting real change is directly proportional to how well you learn and master the system of people you are transforming.

1	It's all PEOPLE SYSTEMS
2	**People FEAR the UNKNOWN**
3	RELATIVITY reduces fear
4	You need SPEED
5	You are writing an EPIC TALE

Tuglus Transformation Law #2:
People Fear the Unknown

One of the greatest challenges in business transformation is getting people to join you on the journey. At every phase, there are people, at all levels of the organization—sometimes the same people, but often not—who will resist. They will deny the need to transform. Avoid participating in the creation of the new world. Balk at learning new processes and tools. Refuse to leverage the real benefits of the changes.

One of the greatest drivers underlying this resistance is the fear of the unknown. You, with your terrifying transformation journey, are introducing a multitude of unknowns into their lives—especially in the early phases where the future state is undefined. We all possess a deep fear of the unknown, which is absolutely understandable. Facing unknowns creates a scary, uncertain feeling that we feel compelled to urgently resolve, even if it is to our detriment. We seek familiar things and predictable outcomes, even when statistics tell us the unknown is a better deal. Even when a significant change in the world threatens the livelihood of your organization, or when the current state of your organization is on an undeniable decline.

We've all heard of people choosing "the devil they know." Sometimes it is said apologetically, with wry acknowledgment that it is perhaps not the best choice. Sometimes it is conveyed as a matter-of-fact statement with a clear implication: *Of course, we choose the devil we know. This is what people do. You can't fault me for it.* In a transformation, this results in people—at all levels—clinging to the old ways instead of embracing the new. Therefore, it is critical to acknowledge this fear and do our best to dispel unknowns along the way in order to reduce it.

When talking about transformation, we often hear that people "fear change." This has always struck me as discordant, a little off-center, not quite right. I have come to realize this is because it is not accurate—it is not the change itself that drives the fear; it's the *unknown*.

We have all been in situations where fear is not only misunderstood but also quickly dismissed. Someone says "people fear change" or "change is hard." Everyone else in the room nods in agreement, and then the meeting moves directly on to another topic. Discussion over. End of subject. *Wait, what just happened?* The implication is that nothing can be done, and it is therefore not worth discussing further.

This assumption is inaccurate and counterproductive. A transformation, by its very definition, requires a substantial amount of change. That is the whole point. As a transformation leader or sponsor, you are always implementing significant, highly valuable changes. You, of course, cannot eliminate change, and if you believe that people fear change as a rule, then you are stuck in the very unfortunate and self-defined position of being the harbinger of fear. In this case, your journey will be very, very lonely. Few people will be brave enough to join you. Expect extraordinarily high levels of resistance. Extreme frustration. And almost certain failure. Your transformation is unlikely to succeed.

Do not let the statement stand. Stating "people fear change" is vastly different from genuinely understanding that people are afraid of the unknown. Do you honestly believe that employees are envisioning a changed job and thinking, "I can't do that" or "This new five-step process will be impossible to learn"? They're not. They quite simply cannot imagine what that new job—or new process or new culture—looks like. Feels like. They cannot see themselves clearly in it. Consequently, they cannot imagine how they will master it, how they will be successful. They worry they might embarrass themselves by being slow to learn, and they wonder if it will create extra work that might be hard to complete in the times expected. They know it will be different, but they don't know *how*. The fear comes from the unknown.

"IT'S THE WAY WE'VE ALWAYS DONE IT"

How often have you heard someone say "it's the way we've always done it" as the rationale for continuing to do something the same way? "The way we've always done it" is familiar and comfortable— not because it is the easiest or best way to operate but because it is a known quantity, an old friend.

I came across a great example of this while shadowing employees who manage insurance claims. I'm sitting down with people at each stage of the claims process in order to understand its current state. This is an extremely customer-focused team, operating with great consistency, but their business processes haven't changed in over a decade.

We begin the tour of the process where claims documents arrive. The team is receiving quite a few documents from customers via physical mail. It appears that paper mail is scanned into digital format by a third party before it gets to the office. "This is great," I think. The mail shows up in an electronic queue, which essentially looks like a list of emails. Employees "work the queue" by opening up the electronic mail, sorting through it, then responding and handing off items as appropriate. Sometimes a customer's insurance claim comes in via this method. When this happens, the employee working the

THE WAY WE'VE ALWAYS DONE IT

① PAPER DOCUMENTS RECEIVED BY MAIL ARE SCANNED IN

② DOCUMENTS ARE PRINTED

③ SUPERVISOR TAKES PAPER DOC TO ASSIGNED EMPLOYEE

④ EMPLOYEE TYPES INFO FROM DOCUMENT INTO A SYSTEM

PAPER ... TO DIGITAL ... TO PAPER... ...TO DIGITAL

queue prints out the claim documents and gives them to a supervisor. "Wait, what?" I think. "Did they just print that out?"

Yes. The mail that had been physically sent through the postal service, then scanned into digital format, is now being printed back out onto paper. "A little inefficient," I think, "but all right, let's follow this document trail and see where it leads."

The printed documents are now in the hands of the claims supervisor. The supervisor chooses a claims specialist to assign the claim to. Then they walk the paper documents over to that person. That claims specialist takes the documents, props them up next to their computer on a little stand, and proceeds to type some of the information from those documents into the claims system.

Catch that? They are now redigitizing the information. To recap, a paper document mailed by a customer had been scanned into electronic format, printed out onto paper again, handed to a supervisor who handed it to another employee, who then redigitized some of the information. Sounds kind of inefficient, right? But it did the job. It was comfortable. You can easily imagine the original process it had grown from, where once upon a time paper mail arrived, was opened and sorted, then physically handed to the appropriate person who would keep all the papers in a file folder for each claim.

I asked why this was the procedure, and the response from employees and supervisors was resoundingly "because we've always done it this way." When pressed further and offered a few improve- ment ideas, they very politely, very respectfully, and *very* firmly assured me that the process worked well and did not need to change. That, in fact, it worked just as well now as it did when it was introduced seventeen years ago. Thank you, but no, there was no need to change.

How often have you experienced this situation? An old, com- fortable process that, when viewed from an outsider's perspective, clearly has a lot of potential to be improved, but insiders seem deter- mined not to change? Expect to encounter many of these during a transformation.

OUTSIDERS HAVE THEIR OWN COMFORT ZONE

You may assume that outsiders are more willing to tackle the unknown than your current employee base. But some outsiders are only eager to transform your organization using the models they know—not necessarily the ones that will deliver the best value to your unique organization.

I know executives who, each time upon arriving at a new company, have been implementing the same organizational model they learned early in their careers, twenty years ago. Again and again. That doesn't mean the model is bad, per se, but I want to draw your attention to the fact that it also doesn't mean it will deliver the best value for you.

"The way we've always done it" is not exclusive to insiders. Consider that carefully as you hire. You must be vigilant—your long-tenured employees are not the only ones fearful of a new paradigm.

The greatest impediment to change, in scenarios like this, is that employees cannot imagine the new way. Even when I described alternatives to the insurance claims team, I was speaking a foreign language. The team couldn't quite imagine it or understand exactly how it would change their jobs. Understandable. Doing anything the same way for seventeen years would make change difficult to envi- sion. For anyone. And so, in a brush with the unknown, they clung to the familiar, the way they had always done it.

IDENTIFY AND DISPEL THE UNKNOWNS TO REDUCE FEAR

Speed is critical in any transformation. And the speed of your business transformation is greatly impacted by how quickly you can get people to take the journey with you. That, in turn, is heavily dependent upon how quickly those people can clearly imagine themselves in the future state.

Throughout a transformation, it is important to actively identify the core unknowns driving fear and dispel them. Allowing these battles to organically unfold without advance preparation can lead to death by a thousand cuts. Each battle will take time, and added together, they can substantially lengthen the time your transformation takes.

"The way we've always done it" is familiar and easy to imagine. It is certain, it is known. The future, well, that is ambiguous. Undefined and uncertain. And therefore frightening. Remember your people system: identifying precisely what is driving human behavior is critical as we lead an organization through a major transformation. In this case, the anticipation and anxiety that comes from an unknown often triggers a fight or flight response, driving bad behavior, resistance, and a strong attachment to the familiar. Your job is to eliminate unknowns, make the unfamiliar familiar, and help people envision the future.

In the claims organization, the notion of having the document remain in digital form was strongly resisted. After lengthy discussion, people began to get more comfortable with the idea. Eventually, the greatest remaining hurdle was a belief that the document needed to be propped up next to the monitor, in order for the claims specialist to easily see the information while typing it into the computer. Ultimately, they were persuaded to test out a process whereby the manager would review and assign the claim without printing it, and the claims specialist would use two monitors so they could see the document on one screen while typing on the other.

Now that it was clear what was to be done, the manager leapt into action. It took a single day to discuss how to procure monitors, what central functions needed to be engaged, and how quickly this could happen. Funnily enough, that evening the manager recalled that there were some monitors in a closet in that very office from a past office consolidation. By the end of the next day, within forty-eight hours of making the decision, a couple of volunteers were set up to test the process. It did not take long for others, once they saw those employees enjoying the setup, to quickly warm up to the new way. Within a month, everyone wanted two monitors and could live without the paper.

This set off a series of further improvements to the process, that those same people were much more willing to engage in. As the proposed changes became easier to imagine, more familiar, more *known*, employees' willingness to change increased. The more familiar they became with proposed changes, and the more visible and clear those changes became, the more it decreased their fear of the unknown. The roadblocks to achieving change were eliminated by eliminating unknowns.

Throughout your transformation, as you notice fear, acknowledge the far-reaching effects it can have. Do not dismiss fear. Actively seek and implement ways to lessen and dispel it. Do this through making the new world—the future state—more familiar. You can do this by:

- Communicating the future state clearly and often across the organization

- Establishing regular communication with people who will be impacted, and in each progressive meeting, striving to dispel a little more of the unknown

- Making parts of the future state real whenever possible by engaging employees to live and test that future state

- Broadly sharing prototypes, designs, and demos of new tools

- Having employees show off future-state processes and tools to other employees

As you travel along the path of transformation, there will be a long stretch of road where the future is undefined. That is normal. You simply have not gotten that far into your journey yet. Initially, bring familiarity to the organization through consistency of communication, and then share future-state information as specific details do become known.

The vast majority of people will be able to change. Expect some difficult people—there are always the troublemakers—and deal with them as you would any poor performers.

There is one special exception. There will be some people who are further along in their careers and who are good team players but will want out. They have thought seriously about the road ahead and would prefer to retire instead of going through another learning curve to master the new world. What to do about that? Expect it. Learn who those people are. Do not treat them like resisters. Figure out how to pull in their expertise where needed, then respectfully exit them out of the organization at a logical time. Have candid conversations with them. Be aware that everyone around them is watching how you treat these people. It will send signals throughout the organization, so be sure to consciously send the signals you want received.

People fear the unknown. Your transformation introduces a lot of change, which will initially be viewed as a huge, scary, amorphous unknown future. To be fair, this is a pretty accurate assessment of it at the beginning. Realize and acknowledge that fear comes from the unknown. Avoid trivializing it or being dismissive, and visibly express confidence in the organization's ability to succeed in the future state. Continuously and visibly turn the unknown future state into something known. Do this throughout the transformation and you will move faster, people will take the journey more willingly, and you won't be so lonely.

Saying "people fear change" is **not** *the same as* **understanding that they are actually afraid of the unknown.**

1	It's all PEOPLE SYSTEMS
2	People FEAR the UNKNOWN
3	**RELATIVITY reduces fear**
4	You need SPEED
5	You are writing an EPIC TALE

Tuglus Transformation Law #3: Relativity Reduces Fear

Everything is relative. This is powerful knowledge when driving organizational change because people assess something new by comparing it to something that is known. When a new model of phone comes out, it is always assessed relative to the current model. If you haven't been to Alaska, you probably imagine the place based on what you've learned on television, the internet, or somewhere you've been that you believe is relatively similar—perhaps Scotland, northern Canada, or Maine. Throughout our lives, all of us are constantly striving to make things more familiar in order to understand them.

Consequently, the framing of a conversation, situation, or challenge will materially affect perceptions and outcomes. The power of relativity is one of my favorite concepts. Let's dive into it. Don't worry, I promise not to bust out any complex mathematical equations. At least not this time.

Let's head back out to the forest to see relativity in action. Imagine you are dropped off deep in the middle of an unfamiliar forest with me. We follow a rough trail and discover what appears to be a lake. I turn to you, and ask, "How long do you think it will take us to hike around that lake? How difficult do you think that trail will be?" What is your answer?

Well, it depends, does it not? Your perception of the situation depends upon your past experience, how relevant you believe that experience to be, and what information has been provided. If you have directly relevant experience—such as having walked around a similarly sized body of water under similar conditions—you will naturally compare it to that. You will feel that you know what to expect from the hike and be able to confidently form an estimate.

If you believe that you have no relevant experience at all, then you may look upon this hike with great trepidation, dreading what appears to be a wholly unfamiliar adventure. In isolation, detached from anything to compare it to, there is no sense of perspective; the situation is entirely unknown. Remember the second law of transformation: people fear the unknown.

I once took a close friend of mine on a hike just like this. Up to that point, this friend had spent his entire life in a large urban area. Even though neither of us had walked this particular trail before, I had been on many other forest hikes and was quite comfortable. Not so for him. It was eye-opening to see how uncomfortable the activity made him, and how much anxiety it created. At one point, I looked back to find him stepping delicately along the trail, trying to avoid contacting any plant with any part of his clothing or body. Lacking any experience with the situation, he had to rely on me for information about how to proceed and how dangerous things really were. (They were not, for the record, dangerous. Though to this very day, opinions may vary.)

For a transformation leader, providing information and expecting people to trust you—no matter how close they are to you or what your track record is—is never as effective as framing a situation relative to something that is familiar to that person. Suppose you have experience that is not exactly the same situation as our forest, but you believe is related—for instance, running long distance on an urban trail. As long as you believe it is related, you will be able to extrapolate from that experience, make assumptions, and form an opinion regarding this journey. Though you will have more anxiety than the person who has hiked a similar trail, you will have far less anxiety than the person who has no related experience at all. And far less anxiety than the person who *believes* they have no related experience at all, which has the same effect.

Throughout your transformation journey, think carefully about

Providing information and expecting people to trust you is never as effective as framing a situation relative to something familiar to that person.

the changes you are leading your organization through. How scary are they? If, in response, you immediately ask "to whom?" and "relative to what?" then you are thinking the right way. It all depends upon what people are comparing it to. The average person has not experienced many corporate transformations, so you should assume that a transformation will initially generate much fear and anxiety. That hike to the other side of the lake is scary, and that destination—your future state—initially appears shrouded in a deep fog of unknowns, making it seem even longer and scarier.

Chances are, if we try, we can often find something familiar to reduce people's anxiety. For example, by pointing out explicitly how parts of a new process are the same, or similar, to parts of the current process. Or by explaining to an employee the ways in which their new role is a lot like the one a close colleague has today. We all find it helpful when someone can describe a new concept by comparing it to something we are familiar with. Or when they can put it into the context of a larger system or situation that is familiar. Any time this new thing

can be conveyed *relative* to something we already understand, we find it reassuring.

Do not underestimate how powerful this can be. Too many transformations fall short when it comes to considering relativity. It is the responsibility of transformation leadership to reduce unknowns, remove the fog, and help people see the path and what lies on the other side. Using relativity requires thoughtful consideration of communications and leaders who truly understand people, but time spent here pays itself back many times over. There are many ways you can incorporate this throughout your transformation journey. For instance, you can compare concepts relative to:

A specific competitor's action: "This is what our competitor did; you can see their new offering online. Like them, we are going to do A and B. Unlike them, we will be doing the following three things that are different in order to position ourselves to gain a competitive edge . . ."

A change that many have been through in the past: "Remember how we made the change two years ago to A? This will be like that, in these ways . . ."

An action made by a company in another industry: "This company in the pharmaceutical industry has implemented an amazing machine-learning and robotics process to develop new drugs significantly faster. You can read about it here. We are going to apply a similar approach to accelerate our new product creation process. It will require us to . . ."

Something another group in the company went through: "This part of what we are doing is very similar to what the product engineering group went through last year. We have some of those team members here today to tell us about it . . ."

Note how the last example involves bringing in speakers from outside the organization. Hearing stories told by people who have gone through a similar experience can be extremely helpful in reducing the unknown. It can also tap into the natural competitive spirit of your organization by helping them think, "If they can do it, so can I." Speakers can come from inside or outside your corporation. The most effective speakers have personally been through business transformation journeys. Pure academics and career consultants are not as effective.

We must connect the dots for people. Even when you communicate things relative to employees' past experiences or something familiar, they may not always make the connection or believe that their experience is relevant. There are rarely precise matches. Therefore, once you identify applicable experiences, you must be very direct in pointing out how those experiences are relevant to the situation.

Relativity is powerful. Use your knowledge of relativity to craft powerful transformation communications. This will reduce fear, which increases willingness to take the journey, thereby increasing the speed of your transformation. And speed is critically important, as we will discuss next, in the fourth law of transformation.

1	It's all PEOPLE SYSTEMS
2	People FEAR the UNKNOWN
3	RELATIVITY reduces fear
4	**You need SPEED**
5	You are writing an EPIC TALE

Tuglus Transformation Law #4: You Need Speed

You need speed. A specific type of speed: not just rapid movement, but focused and productive urgency in action. The world is moving rapidly, savvy competition is running their own plays, and your organization has only so much energy. You have to get this right. You may not have another shot.

So how do we get speed? To move fast, in a productive way that remains focused on real business value, you must have the right transformation know-how.

Right now, across the world, many business-critical endeavors are failing. Acquisitions, mergers, market pivots, new businesses, platform implementations, innovation initiatives—all variety of transformations. What they all have in common is a lack of transformation expertise—the know-how required to pull this off. Without this know-how, timelines drag out, Transformation Programs become easy prey for dragons, and organizations become frequent visitors to common pitfalls. Many simply run out of time to get this right.

The ability to conceptualize and execute business transformations is an extremely advanced, people-savvy, business value-focused, high-stakes form of program management. Sound complex? It is, but by the time you finish this book, you will know what I mean. Simply put, you need the right know-how in order to guide and survive a successful transformation journey. Advanced transformation program fundamentals are necessary in order to design and deliver your future state in a way that produces real business value at the end.

Strong program fundamentals are absolutely required to successfully deliver anything of magnitude. This is so important that some days I am tempted to write a book solely dedicated to program management. But there are already many books and resources out there that no one is taking seriously enough. And to be honest, even though I'm fairly expert in it, I would bore myself to death writing a whole book on the subject. Which is part of the problem. I bet many of you are bored right now even thinking about it. Do not fall asleep. Do not light anything on fire. It's about to get interesting.

Even programs with great vision and solid commitment often fail. Commitment may initially drive activity, but the right know-how channels that into speed with focus. You need next level program management skills to form the machinery that propels the transformation forward, deftly navigating dragons and pitfalls. Strong transformation management does not just manage the work, but manages the people. *All* the people. The people that touch the program in any way, shape, or form. People who are part of the work, people who sponsor the work, people who are loaning resources for the work, people whose jobs are changed by the work, people whose interactions with the company are changed by the work. Are you experiencing a flashback to the first law? Good. It's all about people systems. And your transformation leadership must be geared toward this.

There is a core set of program management skills that any project or program management book will teach you. If I were to ask you why program management fundamentals are so critical, what mission-critical functions they perform, what would you say? Take sixty seconds to think about it.

Most people would say things like this:

- Run meetings, keep people on track, provide status

- Organize and prioritize work, manage capacity and resource utilization

- Manage dependencies

- Manage issues and risks

- Communicate

- Manage politics, tension, and cross-functional conflict

- Secure resources and manage budget, schedule, and scope

- Ensure healthy team dynamics

- Facilitate problem-solving

It all seems important, right? Yes, you absolutely need all of these tasks handled. These are the base program management activities. But they are not enough for a transformation. We need to kick it up a notch. You cannot treat a business transformation like a typical project. Let's get into what that means.

There are three critical next level capabilities that you need in order to successfully navigate a transformation journey, with all its inherent perils and complexities. This advanced set of skills encompasses a level of people-savvy know-how that takes into account organizational attention spans and the changing world around you. The next level capabilities required to successfully lead a transformation are as follows:

Maintain focus on business value. Focus on urgently delivering business value, without a death march, while monitoring the world for new changes.

Foster commitment. Nurture, grow, and maintain the ongoing commitment and engagement of key executives, combatting organizational fatigue, and communicating a compelling tale of transformation.

Predict and engage the people system. Predict behavior of the people system multiple steps into the future, holding people accountable regardless of seniority, removing potential roadblocks to maintain progress, and protecting against time-wasting bureaucracy, circular discussions, and stupid sh*t.

This type of know-how comes from experience. Real experience, inside messy, complex transformations, dealing with dragons, pitfalls, and political perils.

It is all too common for organizations to underestimate the criticality of know-how and shortchange it. Typically, this occurs because leaders do not understand what is needed. "Why can't we just grab any project managers we have in our organization?" they ask, or "Why can't smart people just learn on the job and figure it out as they go?" The answers can be boiled down to one very important reality: In the course of normal operations, this may work for you, but this is a transformation. You need speed. Because you are running out of time.

"Wait," you are thinking. "No way. I just started!" Perhaps you have. It doesn't matter—it is still true. You are already running out of time, the very day you begin your transformation.

Most people are blissfully unaware that as soon as they begin any significant transformation journey, they are fighting against the clock. There are two powerful things that you are up against in this battle: (1) the world, which continues to progress, and (2) inevitable organizational fatigue. Let's take a closer look at both.

POWERFUL THING NUMBER 1: THE WORLD
(STILL MOVING)

You're running out of time. The world is still moving forward, even as your organization is working to catch up. Think about it. Months (or years) of discussion, analysis, and leadership reviews have preceded the start of this transformation. Outside events and trends that were the impetus for this program—competitive threats, changes in consumer behavior, advances in technology, changes in the economy—are still evolving. The world won't stop for your transformation, and so the outputs of your program need to be in place, and generating business value, stat. Which means you must effectively lead your organization through this journey at a brisk pace, while maintaining a strong focus on business value.

Periodically, events in the outside world will spark anxiety and bring into question the value of your transformation. Without strong transformation know-how to maintain commitment and focus, there is the very real risk that your program will be cancelled midstream. Even if the organization desperately needs it.

It's possible that the program should be killed at that point. I am a big fan of killing programs once it is obvious that they will not deliver real value. Then they can have a fresh start if the business case is strong enough. But if a program should be killed, then let's do it based on merit. Do it because a clear cost/benefit assessment has been made, with new information from the changing world, and the expected value is no longer great enough to justify continued investment. Not because weak transformation know-how has led us down this path and forced our hand.

If the value proposition still holds in the face of these events, and leadership is strong, these are simply distractions. But do not underestimate their power. They can be draining. The number of these events you'll experience will increase the longer your transformation effort goes on, and you'll waste more time addressing them. Speed is your friend. Get that value into place fast. You might be able to break up your transformation to deliver value in multiple phases, which can help, but that may not always be possible. Either way, real transformation know-how will provide the speed you need.

POWERFUL THING NUMBER 2: ORGANIZATIONAL FATIGUE

The second powerful thing we're battling is organizational fatigue. This is your company's natural tendency to lose interest, enthusiasm, and engagement over time. Unlike planetary orbiting, this one can be fought off for a while—but you cannot stave it off forever.

Compared to world changes, organizational fatigue is the weaker opponent. It is not an external uncontrollable force, and it grows predictably over time. But given enough time, it too will ultimately win. It simply has greater endurance than you. You must fight vigilantly against it and get to the finish line before it irreparably harms your transformation.

In the beginning, you will have everyone's attention. They will provide the resources you ask for, they will come to your meetings, they will be curious and engaged, asking questions, wanting to make sure you incorporate their needs. That you understand their concerns. As time goes on, attention will be drawn elsewhere, as people switch jobs, retire, become distracted by new things, and get caught up in day-to-day operating challenges. You cannot stop a lot of these things from happening, but with the right know-how you can move fast enough and keep the necessary level of engagement and commitment to complete the journey.

SOMETIMES YOU HAVE TIME TO TRY AGAIN

Do you have time to try again if you fail? Equally important, will you have the energy to try again? Many years ago, I experienced a formidable example of a very large transformation failure, when some of my technology teams were part of a recovery program that restored old processes and technology after a failed transformation. A couple hundred million dollars had been spent erecting a new global platform that was just not working. To unwind the processes and systems, it cost an additional half of that amount. The worst part of it, though, was the fact that the business case was undeniably compelling. Execution, however, had failed spectacularly.

Although this failure was not fatal for the broader corporation, for many companies it would have been. And it certainly reduced enthusiasm to try this again for a very long time. In the meantime, competition was increasing, while years of opportunity were wasted by this organization. Being on the inside, and able to candidly hear about what had happened, was immensely insightful. This was one of the experiences that greatly influenced me as I came to lead larger and broader transformations myself.

For one such transformation, I was brought in to replatform a global insurance business, supporting twenty-eight countries. It was a multiyear, $100M+ endeavor where I led the build out of a new core platform, including organizational changes, process changes, and new technology across operations, finance, accounting, and product. The entire core set of technologies was replaced: a new transactional system, financial system, and data warehouse. When I first engaged in the formulation of the initiative, other executives happily shared war stories of how similar initiatives had been attempted in the past and failed. Why did they fail? Putting technology first instead of people and business process. A lack of experienced transformation leadership. A lack of holistic cross-functional business integration. In summary, weak transformation expertise had struck. They had commitment but had lacked know-how.

They were fortunate in that they could afford to try again. They had time. And they were smart enough to assess what had gone wrong and eventually invest in the right know-how. With a great cross-functional team, I successfully delivered the program, with the promised business benefits. Depending upon your particular situation, and given the decreasing longevity of corporations, you may not have the luxury of another chance. Whether that is because you have run out of chances, waited too long, or are facing serious disruption, you need proper transformation know-how in place from the get-go.

Don't fail for lack of know-how. Transformations are not optional. They *must* be executed to ensure the future success of the company. At the same time, the world continues to move forward, people get tired, and you may not have time for another shot. As soon as you begin your transformation, you are immediately fighting against the clock.

Speed—focused and productive speed—is critical. If this is truly a transformation, and you are serious about it, you cannot assume this can be treated like a typical project, nor can you just throw some smart people at it to learn on the job. You will not be able to move fast enough, in a way that produces the value you need. The right supporting know-how is essential, and now you understand what that means. Throughout this book, you will learn more about this know-how and how to get it.

1	It's all PEOPLE SYSTEMS
2	People FEAR the UNKNOWN
3	RELATIVITY reduces fear
4	You need SPEED
5	**You are writing an EPIC TALE**

Tuglus Transformation Law #5: You are Writing an Epic Tale

Are you writing an epic tale? You should be. Does everyone on the team know they are on a journey to a new land, an exciting place with new opportunities? That they will face perils, dragons, and pitfalls? They should. Furthermore, they should know you are confident that, together, you will prevail in the end.

A business transformation cannot be conducted alone. It involves the well-orchestrated, collective efforts of many people, across many teams, functions, and geographies. It is impossible to understate the impact of strategically crafted, compelling communications when taking people on this journey to a new state.

Everyone should understand how critical this journey is. They must know that they are part of a very important time in the history of this organization. Maybe even an important time in the history of their industry. You have multiple audiences to reach and influence, and slightly different messages for each. There is:

Internal communication to the employees whose lives are being impacted: The employee base must understand the reason for changes. That this is critical to the future of the organization and therefore to their futures. They should expect that the journey will be challenging. They should continually gain clarity of the future state, as unknowns become known. They need to feel confident that they are, and will be, receiving the proper training, direction, and support. They need to feel leadership's confidence in them, in their ability to master this future state. And they must know that they are an important part of achieving the company's success.

Communication to the fearless team executing the transformation: Everyone on the Transformation team must maintain focus on the overarching business goals. They also must feel that they are part of a great team that will come together to take on any challenge, to tackle whatever may come. They must know that this perilous journey is absolutely possible and believe they are certain to emerge in triumph, battle-weary but victorious.

Communication to the executive team and board of directors: Executives must clearly understand and be reminded of their role, and they must be provided information and engagement that maintains their commitment. Board members should feel the clarity of strategy and have confidence in the leadership and direction.

External communication to the public, industry experts, regulators, customers, and others: Customers who are affected by the transformation will need to know what changes are coming their way, why and how this benefits them, and what changes will be required of them. Regulators will want to be assured that the new world will not harm customers or create outsized risk.

A successful business transformation includes a lot of communication. You could start from scratch each time, as you create communications for each situation and audience. However, that would be inefficient and leave you with disconnected stories that will surely come back to haunt you. Dragons looking to derail your transformation will pounce on inconsistencies and highlight them as a reason not to proceed. Many employees will be genuinely confused when they hear different things from different directions.

Let me be clear: I am absolutely not suggesting you create a single set-in-stone presentation deck to be used for every occasion. Not at all. In fact, customize all your presentation materials as you see fit.

I have never found value in enforcing strict templates. Why in the world would you include content for an audience that they neither need nor care about? That is more off-putting than inefficient. You might think you are just wasting a few slides, but you are actually telling that audience that you did not truly think about them when you composed the communication. So customize as needed. Just be sure to build a core story that is shared consistently.

Throughout the journey, we will build the overarching tale of this business transformation. It will share the journey's challenges, perils, and victories. It will share the what, why, how, and when of the transformation. Although you will not have all the information up front—it will build over time—that should not stop you from telling the part of the story that is available at any given time. Specific communications can be built from that, using the most relevant part of the tale for a given time and audience.

Keep top of mind the need to dispel fear along the way. Leverage your knowledge of the second law, "people fear the unknown," and the third law, "relativity reduces fear," to increase the power of your communications. Create familiarity through developing a predictable cadence, including analogies and conveying comparable examples that people are already familiar with, to dispel fear. Share new information regularly as unknowns become known. The goal is not only to communicate information, but also to create familiarity and predictability through this time of great change.

Whenever possible, do this in a way that will engage and energize. "We are going to do that which has never been done before here" is compelling. "It's us against the world" fosters a naturally competitive spirit and is quite effective when true and communicated well. It helps to remind the organization that they are not alone in the world—there are competitors taking their very own transformation journeys right now. Others out in the industry are doubting your organization's ability to succeed—moreover, hoping fervently that you will not—and you will most assuredly prove them wrong.

Transformation is difficult and dangerous, but you are applying the right know-how. You know there will be much planning and coordination and adjusting. You will be tackling the unexpected, mapping new coordinates, and persevering together through dragons and stormy seas. Use your tale to set these expectations across the organization from the very beginning: "We're doing this. We are going in. Prepare yourselves for a wild ride. Anything could happen. And whatever comes, we are confident that we will prevail, to reach the future state and all the benefits it holds."

Be positive in the outcome, but do not paint the journey in overly rosy tones. Going in, everyone should know how epic this will be. If leadership conveys overly optimistic and naïve views regarding what it will really take to do this, then as soon as people understand the reality, morale will tank and the program will be in jeopardy. This is, quite literally, the downfall for some programs. The team may never recover.

You will never overcommunicate during a journey this epic. Throughout the journey of business transformation, the tale is building and expanding. You will adapt and develop many versions of the tale, for different phases of the journey, different audiences, and different purposes. But they will all be born of the same core tale. I will guide you through the first manifestation of your epic tale, the Vision Story, at the end of phase 2 (see page 89), and the second manifestation, the Transformation Story, at the end of phase 3 (see page 135).

Like any leadership vision, your tale must be communicated often. A good foundational story will maintain its core as it is extended throughout the journey. This is your battle cry to bring everyone together—and keep them together—to deliver the vision. Your epic tale tip list:

· You are the narrator.

· Be genuine, engaging, and energizing.

· Think of it as one single overarching tale that you customize for each audience and purpose, choosing to include the most relevant components and the right amount of detail as befits the situation.

· Be confident in the outcome, yet do not minimize or trivialize the challenge.

- Do not worry about overcommunicating. It will never happen.

If you choose not to write a tale, make no mistake, a tale is still being written. And you might not like how it gets told.

People want to be part of something great. Make sure they feel that way. Can everyone on the team tell the tale? Can everyone in the company? And if they can, do they? Make it a tale that everyone wants to tell, and equip them to tell the story.

Have a tale to tell.

Make it epic.

Are you ready to outsmart dragons, leap over life-threatening pitfalls, and perform death-defying acts of transformation? Your initiation is complete. Now that you're equipped with knowledge of the most critical and relevant laws of business transformation, it is time for phase 2, Preparation. Let's recap quickly before heading forward:

1. In the first law of transformation, **It's All People Systems,** you learned to envision a transformation as the architecting or rearchitecting of a system of people. Transformation is all about people, and must avoid exclusively fixating on product, process, or technology.

2. The second law, **People Fear the Unknown,** delved into the greatest force of resistance within that people system, the fear of the unknown. Fear must be dispelled for people to join the transformation journey and move toward the future state.

3. **Relativity Reduces Fear,** the third law, explained how relativity can be used as a powerful force to dispel that fear. This should be applied often.

4. The fourth law, **You Need Speed,** shared why it is so critical to act with urgency and demonstrated the advanced transformation know-how necessary to deliver a transformation with speed.

5. The fifth and final law, **You are Writing an Epic Tale,** discussed how critical it is to be evolving a holistic and compelling story of

transformation, and orchestrating all communications with that at the core.

The better these laws of transformation are internalized, the greater your chances of survival and success. Share them with your entire Transformation team, and more broadly across the organization, so that you are all working from the same guidebook.

The next phase of our journey is Preparation. Which sounds rather harmless, doesn't it? In reality, it can be quite dangerous. The activities in this phase are fairly straightforward, but hidden within this stretch of the journey lie a number of debilitating pitfalls that can limit your transformation's value from the very start.

Are you ready for it? Let's go.

2
Preparation
Preparing Your Organization for Transformation

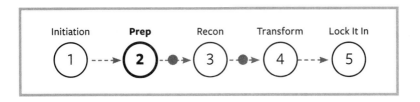

THERE IS A compelling reason for your business to change. You know it, and chances are, many others do as well. But can you articulate it in a way that inspires others to join you on the journey?

Every transformation begins with a high-level vision, a sense of how you believe your future should look and feel. In order to persuade others to take this journey with you, you must validate that vision, support it with facts, and articulate a compelling story around it. From the fifth law of transformation, you learned the importance of taking control of the narrative and telling your own tale of transformation. This phase, Preparation, is about preparing your organization for transformation and getting them to believe in the need for it. Preparation will culminate in the first major manifestation of your epic tale, the Vision Story. Completing this phase entails getting a candid assessment of your organization's current state, demystifying disruption, identifying and catapulting over four common and treacherous pitfalls, and learning what a great transformation leader looks like. By the end, you will have confirmed your belief in the need to transform and be able to convince other key stakeholders of this need as well.

IN THE BEGINNING, A VISION

It all starts with an initial high-level vision. You may already have a vision, but a great transformation vision is backed by data, informed by an honest understanding of two things: (1) the reality of your organization's current state, and (2) the disruption in your world—technological change, social change, and macroeconomic change, as well as competitive activity. Let's take a closer look at both of these.

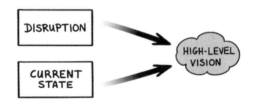

TWO THINGS MUST INFORM YOUR VISION

Assessing Your Current State

A candid assessment of your current state is crucial. How much confidence and clarity do you have regarding your current state situation? Be honest. For example, do you know how much each process costs per item output? How long each type of decision takes? If you're building a new division, do you truly understand what capability, what advantages—and weaknesses—you currently possess, relative to starting that new business?

You need a rigorous and honest understanding of your current state. If you do not have one, go get one. Right now. Seriously, this is something you can requisition immediately. An objective third-party assessment would not be remiss.

To plan your path to somewhere new, you must know where you are starting from. If you begin your transformation with a shallow or overly optimistic understanding of the current state, you will be setting false expectations for the journey. False expectations will lead to unrealistic plans and certain disappointment. Disappointment, in turn, will lead to disillusionment. And disillusionment destroys commitment. Commitment from the employee base, the program team, the executive team, the board—collectively, your people system. And you know what happens without commitment. Game over.

There are two closely related points here, two reasons for fully understanding your current state. First, you cannot plan a route from an unknown starting point. You must truly understand your current reality in order to effectively plan your transformation.

Second, people will not trust your transformation if they do not believe your portrayal of the current state. You must be able to prove that you truly comprehend the reality of that starting point. Do not underestimate the power of candidly acknowledging reality. Demonstrating your comprehension of this reality will gain you trust with your employee base, trust that will lead to a greater willingness to be led through the changes to come.

Consequently, how you talk about the current situation sends a strong message to the organization. If you gloss over the current state, they will look upon the rest of your story with great skepticism. And they *will* know you glossed over it. Because the current state is not wholly unknown. Individually, your employees may not know the entire story, but they each know quite a bit about the reality they work in every day. They know when they are following a process that hasn't been looked at for improvement in over a decade. They know when their competition has better products in the market. They know when profit margins are shrinking. And they read the news and social media. They hear about unhappy investors, see public comments from vocal customers, and track the stock price. Collectively, they are keenly aware of many of the opportunities and challenges facing the company.

If you choose not to be candid about the current state, they will believe one of two things: either you do not understand it, or you have deliberately chosen not to acknowledge it. Either way, you have lost a chance to build trust. Moreover, you have introduced a reason for them to question your credibility and the rest of your story: "Look, they don't even understand what we face today—there is no way I can believe anything after that," they're thinking. And when you ask them to change, it will come up again: "How do we even know this is the right way forward? The leaders clearly have no clue about the current situation," or "That's gonna take a *lot* more effort and time than they think. They have no idea."

When, instead, you candidly face current reality head-on, the impact is dramatically different. People will feel confident that you get it and consequently will assume that you are being honest about the future and what needs to be done.

I experienced a well-executed example of this at Ford Motor Company in 2006. It was a pivotal time for Ford. We underwent a massive restructuring, and there was a lot of uncertainty. Yet we had great confidence that our company would survive the journey and come out stronger, in large part due to the CEO's candid communication of the current state.

When Alan Mulally spoke, he articulated the reality of the current state: he pointed out where we were weak, not performing, not competitive. How our current path was slowly, but surely, putting us out of business. His story was data driven, direct, and to the point. He did not pull any punches. And do you know how that made employees feel? It made us feel like he had openly acknowledged everything we were thinking. That he had done his homework. That he genuinely understood the state of the company. As he laid out the reality of our current state situation, point by point, we found ourselves nodding in agreement.

He continued his story by clearly and concisely depicting the vision for the future we were going to have and the key things we would do to get there. Because of his candor regarding the current state, we believed he was also being honest about what the future state should look like and about what we needed to do. We assumed that these plans were equally data driven and well thought out. That this was all possible. We were instilled with confidence that we could achieve that future, and we were more receptive to listen to the changes that needed to occur. And they were big changes, including big layoffs.

Candor is one of the most powerful tools in a transformation, and it is often underutilized. You must have an honest assessment of your current state in order to plan your journey forward. But then you need to take this information and communicate candidly with your organization. This is a critical component of your Vision Story. Done in a well-organized and thoughtful manner, you will set the right tone, one that increases the willingness of people to join you on your journey.

Do not underestimate the power of candidly acknowledging reality.

Disruption Demystified

Disruption hype is aggressive and pervasive. Messages bombard us from all directions through media and social networks. Conferences, consultants, and technology vendors capitalize upon this: Process Automation! Artificial Intelligence! Blockchain! Quantum! The latest leadership philosophy! Everyone's doing it, you should too! While your competition flails about and chases hot topics as they hit peak hype, let's take advantage of this. Let's harness disruption and put it to work for us.

The world *is* moving forward rapidly, with new concepts and technologies arriving—and reaching useful maturity—faster than ever before. The velocity of technological advancement has been increasing. But many hot topics, from AI to agile, have been around for decades. Many new processes and leadership techniques have roots in things that have been around a while. With a little dedication and the right people, you can get a solid grasp on the disruption, old and new, that your organization faces, and the risks and opportunities contained within. You have the ability to harness all of this and apply it to develop a competitive advantage in the market.

One approach is to dedicate a small group of employees to research disruption. Find a few people who are passionate about keeping up with new trends and tech, who can translate them into the potential for business value, and who communicate well. Then set them loose to discover and report back on the threats, opportunities, and options to take advantage of this in the future.

The reality is that most organizations have a very difficult time finding the right in-house talent that is necessary to conduct a disruption assessment with transformation in mind—the kind of talent that possess the right blend of strategic thinking, holistic industry knowledge, grasp of the specific applicability of disruptive opportunities within the organization, and practical knowledge of transformation. Consequently, most organizations hire a consulting firm. The benefit is that the right external experts will already possess a good grasp on tech and trends. Just be sure to pair them with people on the inside who can best identify the strategic places to leverage this knowledge and will feel ownership for it.

To move through Preparation as quickly as possible, explore disruption concurrent to the assessment of the current state. In a moment, we will talk more about how best to pull the story components together, but before we go there, let's overview the core dynamics of disruption in our fast-moving world. This will provide a framework from which to think about everything your disruption team will be sharing.

NEW TECHNOLOGY IS CONTINUALLY BECOMING CHEAPER AND GETTING TO MARKET FASTER

Technology is advancing rapidly at the micro-level. By micro-level, I mean the components and tools that enable and accelerate everything else. Think of them as the building blocks for everything you see and use. Sensors, microchips, 3D printers, nanotechnology, bioelectronics, new materials, artificial intelligence—these are all enablers. And all are rapidly advancing.

Smaller and cheaper components, combined with open source code, make it easy for anyone to build and test ideas quickly. Sensors, motherboards, and chips are very cheap and easy to assemble. 3D printing continues to advance, with printers continuing to drop in price and a wide variety of materials now available to extrude and print into parts or circuits. Laser cutting, and other cutting and shaping tools, are also appearing in cheaper, portable models that people can buy for their homes.

To put it in perspective, consider the maker community. Makers are people who straddle the edge of art, science, and function. They are coding and building LED dresses. Building personal robots with their friends and kids. Developing prosthetic hands for people who cannot afford them. And rapidly prototyping things to help their communities in times of crisis, like face shields in response to the COVID-19 pandemic. Most of these people have no formal education in coding and technology, yet they fearlessly experiment. They watch some tutorials, make new friends online, buy some parts, share designs, and pick up some Python coding. It's just that accessible, that cheap, that easy.

This means everyone, including you, can afford to build new concepts, quickly prototype, and rapidly test—no matter how big or small, young or old your organization is. Your transformation must take advantage of this and incorporate these possibilities into your future. All you need is the right mindset. And access to information. Which you have.

UBIQUITOUS ACCESS AND HYPERCONNECTION CAN LEAD TO OVERLOAD

People are hyperconnected these days. With unprecedented access to information, myriad social networks, and the widespread availability of public internet, almost anyone has easy access to advice or directions on how to do almost anything. At any time, day or night. Which is great when you want to fix your furnace, get tips on building your own prosthetic, or collaborate with distant friends to build robots at 2 a.m.

The dark side of this connection is overload. Information spreads quickly, and it is hard to control. Shorter attention spans lead to shorter soundbites, which reinforce shorter attention spans. Commercials in six seconds. TV shows refashioned into "video content" with episodes under ten minutes. Social interactions that consist of a single photo. As people find themselves drowning in a world of soundbites, they become overloaded. Too many options lead to customer paralysis.

This means designing customer experiences to simplify processes and avoid paralyzing people. With that in mind, any customer experience should be designed to feel fast and transparent, and consumers must feel in control. Services must be available on demand and digital as much as makes sense.

DESIGNING FOR DISRUPTION

Here is a framework for thinking about customer experience in your transformation. Use it to assess your current state or define your future state. Tailor it as needed for your particular business. Any customer experience should be designed to fulfill the following criteria:

- **In control:** The customer feels in control.

- **On demand:** Customers can interact whenever they want to and need to.

- **Fast:** Interactions feel fast; time does not feel wasted.

- **Transparent:** The experience is straightforward and easy to understand.

- **Digital:** The experience is digital where it makes sense, complementing physical interactions.

TOP TALENT WANTS TO TAKE ON THE WORLD

Take the accessibility of technology, mix in ubiquitous access to information, and add in the hype and romanticization of the start-up world. What do you get? A powerful magnet for top talent. This combined force draws in a multitude of highly talented individuals, especially fresh out of schools. They are starting businesses and joining cutting-edge projects. They are seeking epic journeys with steep learning curves. They are finding opportunities to build new things and change the world.

Many established companies have been trying to tap into that by opening offices in California. Guess what? It's not about your location.

It's about your culture. It's about your story. It's about your opportunities. Great cultures and great opportunities attract great talent. Make sure you consider that in your transformation.

INVESTMENTS ABOUND

Start-up capital is more accessible than ever. Angel investing has gained great awareness and popularity. Accelerators and incubators abound. Traditional venture capitalists as well as corporate venture capitalists continue to invest. Your competitors are investing, sitting on start-up boards, acquiring and integrating new companies. Start-ups are growing up and rapidly becoming viable threats as your newest competitors. Make sure your transformation is taking into account these nontraditional competitors.

THE ENTIRE WORLD IS CONNECTED.
HOW FAST CAN YOU ADAPT?

It's not just social networks. It's supply chains. And economies. Climate and the environment. Health and disease. The entire world is an intricate web of connections, and your organization lives within it. Understanding the core dynamics that impact your organization is critical. From natural disasters to political unrest and pandemics, how could disruption affect you—suddenly or slowly—to offer both opportunities and challenges? Assess how much control you have over what is most important. Consider the flexibility in your processes and technology. How rapidly could you adapt in a crisis? Transform with this in mind. Consciously decide to incorporate the right amount of adaptive capability. The world never sits still. Nor should you.

Face the world head-on. Disruption has direct implications for your transformation vision. The better your understanding of the possibilities surrounding you, the more powerful and compelling your vision will be, and the more value you can design into your transformation. Acknowledge the changes in your industry, which are coming from all directions—the arrival of new capabilities, changing consumer preferences, heavy areas of investment that will produce new competition. Demystify any new hyped-up technology or methodology, and identify the threats and opportunities among them. Understand the global trends that impact you today and those that will likely impact you tomorrow. Know who your competition is and could be, take a careful look at your ability to adapt, and get serious about your game plan to compete.

Don't just keep up. Go on the offensive. Harness disruption.

This all sounds pretty safe so far, right? Not perilous at all. But don't get too comfortable. Dangers lurk nearby. Even with a great understanding of Disruption and the Current State, it is shockingly easy to set a vision that will gain little business value in the end. Four perilous pitfalls lie ahead that can trick you into setting a weak vision. When leaders succumb to them, their organizations become mired and distracted from the market as they drive to complete suboptimal goals. These deadly pitfalls are extremely easy to tumble into, and their disastrous impact is often not obvious until much, much later.

In fact, if you fall into one of these pits, you can set up camp, build a team there, and blindly conduct the rest of your transformation journey from the bottom of the pit. Once an organization adopts the new reality of one of these pitfalls, then even if they successfully navigate the remainder of the transformation journey—which is not trivial—and achieve their goals, the conclusion is tragic. For at the end they discover that they did not create material new value for the organization. That perhaps they are even further behind the competition. Meanwhile, their more transformation-savvy competition, unencumbered by this opportunity cost, has sped past to deliver innovative solutions while they were hanging out in a pit. Don't let this happen to you.

Let's take a close look at these hazardous pitfalls and how to transport yourself—and your entire executive team—safely across.

Pitfall Advisory #1: The Allure of Benchmarking

"All this talk of disruption is overwhelming. Let's just benchmark, and define our future state based on that. Let's just get to parity."

CEO, NOT TO BE NAMED

"Let's just get to parity." Does that seem reasonable to you? Are you nodding in commiseration? Unfortunately, I hear this a lot. Let's break it down and talk about it.

First, let's examine the word *benchmark*. By benchmark, do you mean assess where existing and emerging competitors are investing and changing? That sounds like a great idea. I'm with you. But what is this talk of parity? That second part, where you want to make the benchmark your future state and settle for parity? I'm out. That worries me. A lot. I want you to outperform your competition, not forever strive to catch up with where they've been.

Doing what everyone else has done will keep you behind. You are making a big investment here. Meanwhile, as we know, the world keeps moving. If you always look at where competitors are today and say, "let's just get there," then you will always lag behind. Assuming you even know enough to be able to replicate what a competitor has done (which is a big assumption, given that every organization, including yours, has its own unique environment and people system), then by the time you achieve "there," that competitor has changed and set a new bar. You are still behind. To actually achieve parity, competition would have to freeze. But even if you could freeze the world in place and gain parity, why would you do that? Why expend all that energy, time, and money just to gain parity? No, seriously, this is not a rhetorical question. I really want to know.

Even if you, personally, are not thinking about parity as a goal, I guarantee that someone near you is doing so right now. They are pushing the parity play, and others are nodding in agreement. It might be someone on the executive team, a board member, or a team member who is helping craft the future state. But someone nearby is doing it. There is something in your people system that finds that benchmark strongly attractive.

But why?

In order to combat this common pitfall, I want you to dig deep to understand what is driving this attraction to the benchmark. Think back to the laws of transformation. Is it fear of the unknown? Does a benchmark appear to be a known quantity and therefore less scary? Are people, quite naturally, trying to define the future in terms they can easily imagine, in order to dispel the unknown? Very possible.

Is it attractive because it sounds safe? Perhaps they are thinking it is easier to defend: *If others are doing it, I can explain that more easily.* Politically, in some company cultures, this appears the safer route. And really, it is the same underlying reason—it is easier to define what someone else has done, because it appears more tangible. It seems more *known*. And therefore, less frightening and more palatable. But it is a recipe for disappointment and lost opportunity. Doing something because "everyone else is doing it" is one of the worst ideas in history. And yet, people continue to do this. While it is tempting to dive into the incentive systems that drive executives to waste billions of dollars on what everyone else is doing, that would fill another book. At least. No time for that now. You have more pitfalls to study and a transformation to get to.

Whatever the reason for the attraction to the benchmark—almost certainly related to the fear of the unknown—seek to understand it and acknowledge it so that you can help yourself and others move

forward. I want you to be ahead of much of your competition by the end of your transformation journey. In order to do this, you must build a vision that takes you beyond where you expect the competition to move.

So how to do that? A large part of building a successful vision is understanding and incorporating disruption, as discussed earlier. It seems obvious to look at your own industry for ideas. But look further afield, to other industries, to truly expand your thinking. As discussed in the third law of transformation, it's all relative. Something truly transformative in one industry may be table stakes in another—and easily leveraged.

If you look carefully, you can find patterns of disruptive concepts spreading across industries. For instance, consider transportation, retail clothing, and food, three industries that are quite different. A pattern that has spread across all three is the concept of providing consumers access to luxury services in affordable increments, powered by advanced algorithms and machine learning. It has led to the emergence of new players in each area: personal driver services through ride-sharing companies such as Uber and Lyft; personal stylist services through companies such as Stitch Fix; personal chef services through high-quality meal delivery plans such as Blue Apron and Hello Fresh.

This is just one example of disruptive opportunities that have traveled across industries. You, too, can take advantage of another industry's advances. In fact, this can be far more powerful than you may realize. These companies are not your direct competitors, so they may be more willing to share information and openly discuss their transformation journey with you. Those ideas have already been brought to life in another industry, making them more knowable. Less unknown. Therefore less frightening, if you will recall from the second law, *people fear the unknown.*

Be brave. You cannot freeze the world. Evolution continues. Technology advances. Consumers change. Right now, your most dangerous competition is quietly working on advancing their position. Benchmarking is interesting, but it is not nearly enough. It is just another piece of data to consider. Go ahead and get some competitive intel, do some benchmarking. But meanwhile, think bigger. Broader. Bolder.

Pitfall Advisory #2: Just Technology, Please

"All I need is a new technology platform."
DIVISIONAL HEAD, NOT TO BE NAMED

This deceptively simple statement, though misguided, is used with dangerous regularity to form the basis of a transformation vision. At first glance, it appears quite rational. Sometimes the technology underpinning our business is ancient and we just need to modernize.

Right? OK. Sure. Maybe. But isn't that a bit narrowly focused? If you accept that as fact and follow it to its natural conclusion, then you will have only replicated your existing way of business with a shinier tool. And while doing so, wasted an opportunity to truly build business value.

Imagine the following conversation, between the chief technology & information officer and the chief executive officer, that plays out every day in boardrooms across the world:

CTIO: Our over-twenty-year-old infrastructure and software, running our entire core business, has reached its useful limit. We've been holding it together for a while now, but we must urgently replace it or [insert really bad things that will happen here].

CEO 1: Sounds expensive. Find a way to extend what we have.

The same conversation, with another CEO, might play out with another common response:

CEO 2: We've been putting it off for a long time. I guess we need to do it.

Common answers. Neither good. In fact, the CTIO's pitch isn't so great either. They are not having the right conversation. By itself, the existence of new technology is *not* enough to justify the investment for a full-blown new platform. Regardless of how many trendy words are included—cloud, agile, AI, DevOps, edge. You know what I'm talking about. At best, we are back to "everyone's doing it" and chasing parity. Which we just talked about. But let me refresh your memory: it's a bad idea. But the new platform will be cheaper to run, you say? Still not good enough.

This is a serious consideration. There will always be newer, better technology available. And it will not be cheap. If this is a significant transformation in a small to mid-sized company, we could be talking an investment of millions or tens of millions of dollars. Maybe a hundred million. If this is a large company, we are talking hundreds of millions of dollars. Furthermore, a large transformation is a multiyear endeavor that will engage many employees, pulling them away from other activities.

Meanwhile, as they spend a significant amount of time and money on this, the world is still changing. They are missing a big opportunity to deliver greater business value, to meaningfully move the company forward.

This is still true even if this appears to be a small transformation. Maybe you don't think this is a problem. Maybe your business can sustain a wasted year. Or two. Or three. But why should you?

The CEO and CTIO are having the wrong conversation. The proposal, as it stands, is poorly framed and the answers are shallow. It is time to step back and reframe. This "technology first" approach is tactical and myopic. A strategic approach is needed. I have held executive roles on both sides of the business/technology divide, both heading business operations as well as heading up the technology function. I fully understand where both sides are coming from. And I will definitively state—at the risk of starting a fight with some of my CTIO friends (and some business leaders as well)—that an aging technology stack is not a good enough reason alone to make this investment.

Technology leaders, I know you are frustrated. Your burning platform, your case for change, foretells dark days ahead. And it seems to you, that unless there appears to be a crisis, you will not get traction for a much-needed technology upgrade. CEOs and divisional leaders are also frustrated. That technology story sounds scary, for sure, but it is disconnected from business value and strategy. Technology stories that stand alone fail to connect to the true needs of the business and deliver meaningful change. Major investments, to be transformative, must take advantage of disruption and opportunities on multiple fronts, not just in technology. They must move the company forward in a material, competitive way.

Outside of sticker shock, this is why business leaders find themselves dragging their feet to approve a tech-centric proposal. This is also why, after an organization has implemented one of these technology-obsessed programs, no business leader seems to care, even if it was delivered perfectly (which is rare).

Large technology replacements should always be in concert with strategies and business activities to drive business value. An aging technology stack is nothing more than an input to your current state analysis. Perhaps an important input, but still just an input.

Back to the conversation at hand. Let's spring across this pitfall. Suppose you are the CEO. What do you say to your CTIO?

> CEO 3: Thank you for this thoughtful analysis. I'd like to see this framed into the greater strategic direction of our company. Please work closely with the heads of these business areas and go deep into their vision to make us a powerhouse in our industry. Come back with a proposal for how we will achieve those goals with the right enabling technology.

If you are the CEO, it is now clear what you should do. If you are the transformation sponsor or leader, it should also be clear: make sure that the transformation vision you develop provides a strategic advantage to your organization that is far greater than a pure technology replacement program. Do not let your organization fall prey to this pitfall.

The truly unfortunate thing about "technology first" investments is that no one is happy in the end. When successfully implemented, they are nothing exciting, because there is no material impact in terms of business value. When they fail to implement well, they become a major distraction and a drain on resources.

Sometimes the pitfall proposal is not coming from the technology team, but from a business executive. Some leaders, both business and technology leaders, believe technology is a solution in and of itself. Some even believe that technology alone can transform a business process, without reengineering the system of people surrounding it. That is another fun pitfall. Let's visit that one next.

Pitfall Advisory #3: Technology as a Magic Process Fix

"Technology will fix my process."
BUSINESS EXECUTIVE, NOT TO BE NAMED

You may be smiling right now. Because you've been there. You've seen this. To the uneducated, it appears the easy solution:

> Business leader: My process is inefficient. We'll just get one of these newfangled systems with artificial intelligence and automation, throw it in the cloud, and we will be catapulted into a new world of rainbows and unicorns and material improvements in efficiency. Those technology vendors and consultants certainly make it sound easy. And, as they like to tell me, everyone else is doing it.

By now, you know exactly how I feel about "everyone else is doing it." So, I won't rehash that. It's a bad reason, though. Really bad.

Feel up for some fieldwork? Attend any technology conference. Randomly approach a person. Ask them if they have ever experienced a technology implementation that failed to change the actual business because it focused purely on the technology. They will almost certainly say, "Yes, let me tell you about the time . . ." When you have heard their story, choose another person. Repeat. And another. I guarantee every single person will have a story like this.

While you are at the conference, humor me with one more activity: Seek out some people employed by large technology vendors. Tell them you are new to technology and that you are learning. Ask about the most disappointing technology implementations they have done for clients. Ask about the greatest challenges. Ask what business leadership expected the technology to solve.

Listen closely. Wait for it . . .

Wait for them to complain that the client's leadership expected technology to solve a process challenge. That putting in a new software system didn't increase the production line's output because the employees were not engaged effectively. That investing in a huge data lake did not generate meaningful business insights. That some other expensive technology system has been implemented but is still seeking a business need that will prove its value. That the technology could have done *so much more*, if only...

If only the client had set clear business goals up front. If only they'd redesigned their processes first. If only the client had put more effort toward maximizing the value of the technology, in conjunction with people and processes, instead of just implementing it. If only they'd invested in more—or any—organizational change management. But unfortunately, it was a struggle to get the business to put in the necessary effort to maximize the value of the technology. To take ownership. To connect it into the people system. Most of the stories will lead there. Unfortunately, this is a very common occurrence.

It is worth noting that an organization is not always led into this pitfall by a business leader. Sometimes it comes from a technology leader. Or a consultant. Be vigilant. No matter where it comes from, don't fall for it. Challenge it and adjust.

The vision you set for your transformation must not assume that technology alone will improve a process. People must be taken on a journey, and behaviors must be changed. "Technology only" implementations that fail to take into account the people system will not effectively fix a process. They will not drive real business value. When a transformation vision assumes that technology will magically transform a process by its very existence, the organization is being set up for limited business value achievement in the end. But people will try. It happens all the time. It doesn't have to happen to you.

Pitfall Advisory #4: Centralize It All

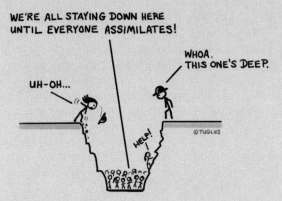

"It's hard to communicate across the business units. Especially our global subsidiaries. We just need to centralize it all. Get to one core system, one platform."

BUSINESS EXECUTIVE WITH TEAMS SPREAD ACROSS THE WORLD, NOT TO BE NAMED

So, you think you want to centralize your business. Or some portion of it. Perhaps your product platform, or the finance and accounting operations. Maybe your administrative functions. Maybe you want to bring some of your divisions into the corporate matrix of central functions. Your vision is clear: centralize it all.

Stop. Before you proceed any further with that line of thinking, be honest with yourself—what do you really want to achieve? What is the real business value you are seeking? Is this the only way to get it? How long will it take (for real)? How much is achieving the value dependent upon people changing their behaviors? Is the benefit still there once you factor in all the people system considerations? And, by the way, just out of curiosity, does centralization happen to be trendy right now?

To be able to get the entirety of an operation onto a single platform—including that painful last 10 or 20 percent that requires outsized effort—was once widely considered a badge of honor among technology and operations leaders. (Maybe it still is in some circles.) It was widely regarded as a very difficult accomplishment and commonly understood to be a good thing to have centralized it all. Executive recruiters would pounce on it in interviews. "Did you *really* get all the business units onto a single platform?" they would say, with a smirk and raised eyebrows. Well, yes. Yes, I did, actually. And, I have to say, in retrospect, it is not something to aspire to. Unless it really, truly makes sense for your organization.

The decision had already been made to centralize core operating processes and systems onto a new platform by the time I arrived on the scene. I must confess to not questioning it too deeply at the time. It didn't seem like a bad idea to have this global, multidivisional company operating as one. But was it really worth it? A few years after successfully launching the new core operations supporting twenty-eight countries onto the same platform, the decision was made to sell a number of business units. At which point, I became the lucky person who got to negotiate the separation of that platform. Because past centralization efforts are a sunk cost at the time you are divesting a business, they do not become visible. But I knew how much time, money, and energy had been put into getting to the centralized state of a common operating and product platform. And I learned quickly that as a subsidiary is separated, those companies often find their platforms too expensive for them to run alone or are encouraged to migrate to new processes and tools by their new owner. All this caused me to really think hard about centralization going forward.

I want you to think hard about this strategy as well. First of all, centralization is costly. It takes time, energy, and money. Taken too far, centralization results in bureaucracy that limits innovation, speed, and flexibility. In people terms—because, do not forget, it is all about people—it can stifle initiative and destroy ownership. On the other hand, a highly distributed model, with many independent entities, has its own serious weaknesses. Most notably, operating many separate divisions limits synergy across groups, loses out on economies of scale, and limits corporate control. In a perfect world, we want flexibility, innovation, and synergy with some intelligent economies of scale where it makes sense. And just the right amount of control.

Companies tend to swing back and forth over time, centralizing and decentralizing various aspects of their business. They move too far in one direction, or more commonly, new leadership arrives, and they're off on a mission to reach the other side again. Centralize. Decentralize. Centralize. Decentralize. Buy some companies. Leave them alone. *Wait, what did that division do without telling us? We need control. Let's integrate them. Hm, we've decided to sell them. Gotta separate them first... why did we fold them in so closely to the rest of the business?* Decentralize.

It all seems like an awful lot of wasted time and money. Time and money that could have been better spent elsewhere. The opportunity cost concerns me more than the financial cost. Remember our discussion about disruption? The world is moving, and you don't have time for these games.

It is important to think carefully about integration and centralization. Do not assume that centralization is, solely, a good thing. Is the dream to easily share product models and assembly data? You might need common data definitions, templates, and a sharing mechanism that all global product teams are taught to use. But it may be wasteful to build and enforce a completely identical process and a single software system to run all products. The real question is not centralized versus decentralized. The real question to ask is: How far should we integrate, and where? There is no one right answer, as it depends on your organization's unique strategy and the anticipated business value.

Speaking of anticipated business value, this is where I want you to stop and think carefully. Make sure you are truly making moves to gain value. Blindly assuming centralization is good, and that it will solve your problems, is a dangerous and surprisingly common pitfall. The same holds for keeping everything separate. Unless, of course, you have a deliberate holding company strategy. But typically, you have bought or built organizations in order to extend your existing competitive reach in some way. As such, keeping them totally separate does not make sense. But neither does heavily centralizing.

When you work in an organization that has distributed business units, multiple geographic locations, or a number of acquisitions, the question of centralization will arise periodically. The trick is to objectively focus on business value to the best of your abilities and avoid wasting resources running to one extreme or another. When you set your transformation vision, consider the following: What are you really trying to achieve? What are the different ways to get it? What are the pros and cons of each? Lay that out on a single page. Then create a list of other transformative things important to the organization. Compare. Is it really important to centralize? If so, how much and in what ways will it achieve real value? Do not just assume centralizing is the answer.

The Transformation Leader

You are planning widespread change, cutting across functions and countries, overhauling entire businesses, dramatically advancing your technological capabilities, and potentially betting the future of the organization on this initiative. I get it, I've lived it. It is big and messy and scary. And it will impact your future greatly. There is a lot at stake.

If you are like most transformation sponsors, you have only a vague idea of what a good transformation leader looks like. And if you are the designated transformation leader, you may not be aware of what traits are most critical to your success. This section will define what a great transformation leader looks like to help you hire one or assess yourself.

For sponsors, investing in the right transformation leadership talent is crucial. Now that you have decided to get serious about transformation and have acknowledged the need for a high-caliber transformation leader, you will have to find one. For the most complex and wide-reaching transformations, you will be seeking an executive-level leader. For those situations where you are only transforming a small portion of your organization, you may be seeking a leader beneath the executive level. At any level, finding a leader can be difficult.

Regardless of whether you are seeking an executive, manager, or anything in between, this is a unique role that requires a unique individual. Chances are, you do not have a lot of experience hiring transformation leaders. Unfortunately, even professional recruiters find this challenging. Consequently, it is very important that you understand what you are looking for so that you get what you need.

The following guidance is written with the most senior transformation leader in mind. Even if you are not seeking an executive, this guidance will help you identify and hire the right leader. Seek out the same characteristics, and scale down the seniority of leader to match your needs. If you decide to choose an internal, top talent individual and appoint them to lead your transformation, be sure to set them up for success and not frustration: They must possess the characteristics of a transformation leader, which I am about to detail. And they must be provided the support of an experienced transformation coach.

If you, yourself, have been appointed to lead the transformation, this guidance can help as well. Use it to identify and recruit the program managers for your core team. Use it to understand what is expected of you. It will also help you reflect upon your own strengths and the gaps you may have. Do not be afraid to ask for the support you need. This is absolutely not the time to pretend you have all the answers. Really, it is very rarely the time for that, but right now it will be deadly. It will come back to haunt you. Demand a coach if you need one.

Executive sponsors, it is tempting to give this opportunity to someone you are familiar with. Someone who makes you comfortable, even if they have little to no background in this, no real experience running even part of a program of this complexity and magnitude. After all, you, yourself, are human and not immune to the second law, the fear of the unknown. You too are attracted to the known, the familiar. However, I cannot stress enough just how important it is, right now, not to move toward your comfort zone. Resist its magnetic attraction! This is the top job in your mission-critical transformation. This is not the time to give someone a "career growth opportunity" or a "stretch assignment." It is not the time to give it to someone because "they're a good guy." (Is there ever a good time for that?)

You want to develop internal talent? Love it. Here are some ways you can do it. Once the transformation leader drafts their program team, add a few roles, at different levels, for talent development. We'll talk more about leveraging existing corporate talent later.

HOW TO IDENTIFY A GREAT TRANSFORMATION LEADER

Good transformation leaders rarely fit into standard recruiting boxes. Let's profile this rarity.

Outstanding orchestrator: Above all this person is an outstanding orchestrator. A business architect. They can juggle many complex, disparate things in their head—people, processes, geographic differences, interdependencies, risks, politics, socioeconomic threats and opportunities, and more. They are great at creating shape and structure out of ambiguity and complexity, building logical workstreams out of the multitude of activities required. Workstreams that continuously forge toward the goals in concert with other connected activities. At the same time, they are extremely adaptable. They can adjust for any challenge. They constantly scan the horizon, envisioning potential pitfalls long before they occur and preventing them. And they do all of this while keeping intense focus on the goals that will drive business value.

Straightforward communicator: This person can articulate the transformation vision in a way that anyone can understand. They avoid jargon and simplify complex concepts. They are skilled at seeing the world from the perspective of others—both executives and employees—and this enables them to communicate well across functions and countries. You also won't hear them sugarcoat anything. They are straightforward communicators and not particularly impressed with stripes or titles. Critically, they hold everyone accountable for their part in the transformation, whether those people report to them or not, regardless of a person's level or status in the organization.

Takes ownership, acts autonomously, and empowers teams: A great transformation leader does not behave hierarchically. They have their goal, and they are not messing around. They know there is no time for playing games. Naturally confident in operating with autonomy, authority, and taking ownership, they instill this conduct in a great leadership team that they assemble (through a combination of both external and internal hires) and genuinely empower while they themselves actively play their orchestration role.

Calm in a crisis, determined, persistent, fearless: New information and challenges appear often during a transformation journey, but they will not throw this person off-kilter. Unexpected information is considered, incorporated into their mental model, and then built into the program. When a team member informs them that something is not working as anticipated, they do not get angry, upset, or stressed out. They get focused. They are in their element. Diving in to help the team frame their problem, and guiding them to discover options and solve it. Supporting, facilitating, and enlisting outside help when needed. Constantly scanning the world to find a way to make things possible. They are not afraid to adapt, shift activities, or replan a program when an overwhelming amount of new information has come into play. This leader is adept at considering implications, adjusting, and reshaping the teams. They are determined to deliver the envisioned future. Persistent. Fearless.

Now we know what they look like. Most of these characteristics will not show up on a resume. So now let's talk about the things that will, so you can convey that to your executive search professional and your human resources leader.

WHAT YOU DO (AND DO NOT) NEED IN YOUR TRANSFORMATION LEADER

Because a good transformation leader is rare, it is important to clearly identify what skills and experience are truly required—and what is not. You need the characteristics detailed above, absolutely. But as you create your position profile, and add additional criteria, do not create a laundry list with every single facet of the perfect candidate. That is a mythical creature. Be honest about what is nice to have and what is essential. If you try to create the perfect, all-inclusive description, you will attract the wrong candidates. By the way, those job postings that seek mythical creatures are also hurting your ability to find diverse candidates. So, what other clues beyond the characteristics we have detailed will help you identify great candidates?

You need to find an experienced leader who has delivered transformations and who has done so in environments of similar or greater complexity to yours. Therefore, you must identify your critical complexity factors. What do I mean by complexity factors? Maybe you are planning a cross-functional transformation in a heavily matrixed environment. Or a global transformation across twenty countries of independently operating business units. It could be you are an entrepreneurial company with a very technical product set. Highly regulated industry? Engineering culture? Nonprofit? Pick three or four complexity factors like these, the ones that you feel are most critical. These form the foundation of the experience you are seeking. While tempting to add all the complexity factors you can think of, keep in mind that this person will be hard to find, so do not make it impossible.

As you are doing this, you may be writing down your industry as one of your factors. You shouldn't be. Specific industry knowledge may be required in some roles, but definitely not this one. You absolutely *do not* need someone with experience in your industry. In fact, that may be more harmful in the end. It is often advantageous to bring in someone who has not worked in your industry. An outsider will naturally challenge your company's assumed truths, finding possibilities beyond the legacy belief that things must continue to be done the way they always have.

When I was new to the insurance industry, I cannot count how many times someone told me something was not possible, something that when I asked to understand further, was discovered to be absolutely possible. My favorite assumed truths were "legal won't let us," or "we can't do that due to regulation," because those were the easiest to prove or disprove. Sometimes information was simply outdated and regulations had changed. Surprisingly often, though, the "truth" was nothing more than a tale, rooted in misunderstanding, passed down through many employees over many years, that everyone now believed. One that had never been true.

You do not need perfect industry and functional fit. What you need is for them to be able to quickly identify and understand the core dynamics of your business. Do this by seeking comparable complexity experience. Similarly, while it seems logical to seek experience in the exact same size of company (or some people like to seek "the same or larger"), that is also not the priority many people believe it to be. The size of the organization a candidate has worked for is nowhere near as important as the complexity of the transformation they have handled.

For instance, a common need is for a leader who has experience building and maintaining strong relationships, with diverse groups, remotely. Companies are often widely distributed, encompassing different cultural norms, working styles, and time zones. Civil unrest, natural disasters, pandemics, and other crises add further complexity. If this is your need, seek someone who has executed at least one transformation with this complexity factor—they should be perfectly comfortable building rapport and holding others accountable remotely, across time zones and microcultures. If this is important to you, experience leading transformation in a smaller but heavily distributed and global company can be more valuable than experience in a large company that houses all of its employees in very few locations.

How do you articulate all of this on a position posting? Suppose you are in a highly regulated industry, and you have decided that is a key complexity factor for your leader. Include "experience in a highly regulated industry" in the description. Not "must have banking experience" or "must have energy industry experience" or "must have pharmaceutical experience." This is not a search for a subject matter expert. You need to find the orchestrator, the ringleader, the mastermind. The fearless leader who can take an organization from concept to reality. You need this core skillset in your leader far more than you need them to know exactly how your company and industry have always done things.

Furthermore, let me share a secret about these people: the best transformation leaders have no interest in solving the exact same challenge again. They thrive off the journey and the diversity of challenge inherent to every transformation. They are not looking for predictability. Remember, they are in their element when shaping chaos and turning concepts into reality. So, if you post a very specific job description, seeking a person who has previously done exactly the same transformation—in the same industry, company size, functions, geographies, products—then do not be surprised when you cannot find any good candidates. If someone comes to you and says, "I've done exactly that before, in precisely the same type of environment, and I want to do it again," be skeptical. Be ready to ask a lot of questions to make sure they really are the right kind of person.

WHEN DO I HIRE?

The perfect time to onboard your transformation leader is right now, during the Preparation phase, while the current state and disruption studies are being conducted. Start searching as soon as possible. It may take a while to find the right person. Ideally, they join your organization before the studies are completed, and while that work is underway, this new leader can begin immersing themself in your business. Learning your organization's culture, history, and idiosyncrasies. Meeting other members of the executive team and building rapport. Shadowing key functions.

Bringing an experienced transformation leader into the mix early can add credibility and inform your communications to the board. This person possesses the expertise to make transformation real to people, to help them both imagine a future and feel that it is possible to achieve. This leader will tackle one of the greatest challenges in getting a transformation off the starting line: the executive team's fear of the unknown. More likely than not, your executive team has limited transformation experience, making it difficult to imagine how such an expansive endeavor will actually occur. Therefore, it is difficult for them to imagine how it will succeed. As we have discussed, fear of the unknown, conscious or subconscious, creates attachment to the familiar, which in turn generates resistance to change. If you find yourself in analysis paralysis, demanding more and more information, perpetually postponing commitment to begin, this may be the root cause.

If you cannot persuade yourself to hire a full-time transformation leader yet, consider hiring a part-time advisor for six months to help get you through the creation of the Vision Story (see page 89). Get help if you need it. You cannot afford to linger. The world is continuing to move forward and change around you.

You Can't Outsource Ownership

People are busy. No one wants to give up their staff. They can't seem to stop anything they are doing in order to invest in the future. So why not just hire consultants? This question comes up all the time.

While you can outsource work, you absolutely cannot outsource ownership.

Companies have become quite adept at retaining only core competencies in house, and they regularly rely on outside support for many tasks. Almost certainly, you will not have the capacity and capabilities required to conduct all of your transformation activities with internal resources. That being said, there are some very important places where you *must* invest in internal staff—the right internal staff. Consultants can be leveraged in many ways throughout your transformation journey, but they cannot do everything for you. To deploy them successfully requires understanding that while you can outsource work, you absolutely cannot outsource ownership.

With the right internal oversight and partnership, consultants can be applied quite effectively during a transformation. They can often assemble teams faster than you, provide capabilities that your organization lacks, and step in where you have a short supply of talent. However, no matter how great your consulting partner is, in order to leverage them successfully, you must establish the right internal mindset and support within your organization. Without this, your consultant's work will only create the perception of progress and will ultimately produce little business value. This happens way too often, resulting in frustration and blame, with neither you nor the consulting firm happy with the outcome. Guess what? It's not your consultant's fault. The ownership and accountability reside with you.

You know this. And in the case of a transformation, acknowledging and living this ownership is especially crucial.

Below are some general guidelines for engaging consultants in a transformation. Following that, I will discuss outsourcing considerations particular to this phase of the journey. In later chapters, I will address the outsourcing considerations related to other phases of the journey.

Transformation ownership: The executive sponsor and the transformation leader are accountable for the success or failure of this transformation. Period. The transformation leader is dedicated to this full time.

Transformation leadership: Consultants and vendors, regardless of their expertise or the size of the engagement, do not reduce the need for strong transformation leadership. Be sure to retain strong internal ownership and accountability in not only the role of the transformation leader, but also the team directly reporting to the transformation leader. All of these people should be full-time employees.

Subject matter experts: The right amount of time—and it may be significant—must be allocated for participation of all necessary subject matter experts. Only your expert employees really know how your business works.

In short, key leadership and subject matter expert roles should be filled by employees, and regardless of what work may be outsourced, *ownership* can never be outsourced. Let's look at potential areas for consultants in this current phase: the current state assessment and the disruption assessment.

CONSULTANTS FOR THE CURRENT STATE ASSESSMENT

You may choose to hire a consulting firm to conduct the current state assessment. Alternatively, you could form a full-time special project team of employees. But it is perfectly reasonable to outsource this effort. As I mentioned earlier, the benefit of an external party is in providing a more objective analysis than many internal teams would. The downside is that the consultants may be more trusting of the information they receive, taking it at face value. This means they often do not know where or how to dive deeper, or are not provided the incentive to do so. Of course, that all depends greatly upon the caliber of consulting team you receive. This potential weakness can be mitigated by choosing your consultants carefully and by creating strong internal ownership that guides the work.

When going the consulting route, assign clear ownership: a senior leader in your organization should be assigned ownership for the current state analysis, be responsible for working with the consulting firm, and be expected to stand behind the output. It is also important to focus the effort on gathering facts about the business that relate directly to the type of business value you want to achieve. How long do processes take today, such as the fulfillment of an order? Or to onboard a customer? What are all the costs for each business activity? What are the ages and version of each tool? What level of flexibility do core tools and processes have? What specific potential for synergy exists with current businesses?

Consultants can also provide benchmarks. But do not forget, we are not going to make those benchmarks our goals! They are only data inputs. If you find yourself tempted, go back and review Pitfall Advisory #1 (see page 64). It is much too easy to fall into that trap. You're going to be smarter than that.

CONSULTANTS FOR THE DISRUPTION ASSESSMENT

As with the current state assessment, consultants can be excellent resources for providing a disruption assessment. The right consultants will already be knowledgeable about disruption and have exposure to multiple industries. Ask for specific actionable information and forecasts, not just generalities. For example, AI-enabled digital chatbots are at what level of maturity? Where will they be in three years? Where could we apply them? And what are the key considerations when implementing them in our particular business?

Similarly, when the consultants assess your competition, keep in mind that it is nice to know where the competition is today, but it is even more important to know what that competition is likely to do in the next three to five years. Make sure they provide opinions on potential entrants as well as existing competitors.

Most companies stop here. They requisition the report; the consultants do their disruption research, typically without much involvement from you and your team; then you get the debrief, read the report, and move on from there. Disruption assessed. But I suggest one more step to get the most value from this. Before widely reviewing the results from the consultants, assign an internal team of business experts—those people who really understand how the core of the business operates and makes money—to read the report and provide their own interpretation and recommendations based on their knowledge of the organization and industry. Give them just a week or two. Their goal is not to change anything in the report, but to supplement the consultants' report, generating additional specific thoughts on how disruption offers opportunities and threats to your unique organization. In most cases, they will be able to add some great insights. Then present and review both reports—the consultants' report plus the supplemental insiders' assessment—at the same time.

Again, the output and guidance that is produced must be clearly owned by a senior leader. You cannot outsource ownership. This principle holds true throughout a transformation, but it will become particularly critical to take to heart in the next phase of the journey, the Reconnaissance Mission.

It's time to tell a story. You have completed your preparation work, executed solid research and analysis, studied and skirted some dangerous pitfalls, and learned how to hire a great transformation leader. More than ever, you are convinced of the need to change, and you are beginning to imagine the future. By this point, you have evolved your initial thoughts regarding your transformation vision, validating and adapting as you delved into your current state situation and the disruption in your world. Now it is time to bring it all together in your Vision Story, which will help you begin setting expectations and gaining support across the executive team and, as applicable, the board of directors.

Vision Story

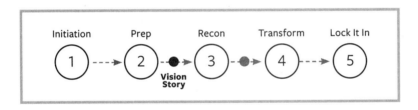

Initiation — Prep — Recon — Transform — Lock It In

1 - - - ➤ 2 - •➤ 3 - •➤ 4 - - - ➤ 5

Vision
Story

EXPLORATION INTO current state and disruption have made you even more convinced of the need to change. It is time to share this conviction. You cannot succeed if you are the only one who believes. Let's compose your Vision Story, the first major manifestation of your epic tale, and the vehicle by which you build a broader belief in the need to change. Executive sponsors, this is your story to tell. Transformation leaders, you, too, must be a skilled orator of this story.

Before we do that, take a moment to confirm that you are ready for this by checking that Preparation is complete. Is the current state well understood? Check. Has disruption been satisfactorily assessed for both opportunities and threats? Check. Have you evolved your vision, if necessary, given what you have learned? Excellent. Now, look around and confirm you are not stuck in a pit. Have you fallen into any of the four pitfalls common to the Preparation phase? Or did you catapult across in a death-defying feat of transformation?

Once you are certain that you have safely crossed those chasms, and maintain a strong belief in the need for transformation, then you are ready to move forward and articulate your Vision Story. Let's take a look at how to build it.

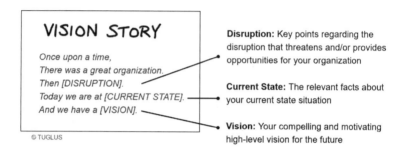

The Vision Story has a very clear purpose: to build belief in the need to transform. It is constructed by combining a candid picture of the current state with insights regarding disruptive threats and opportunities to offer a compelling vision of what the future state could, and should, be. This story is told by the executive sponsor and the transformation leader, and the audience is typically the executive team and the board of directors. The components of this story are clearly laid out in the figure above.

This is the elevator pitch version of the story—the short, concise version you can use to tell anyone why this transformation must occur. In addition, you will almost certainly want to build a longer slide deck or video to guide a more formal conversation. Include key current state data points, demonstrate applicable core processes that need to change, and include the most relevant details of disruption, both threatening and opportunistic. If you have any compelling demos or physical examples that will make it real to the audience, be sure to employ those as well.

Go ahead, build energy and excitement. Let your confidence in this vision show. You need to persuade people to join you; you need them to believe that this transformation must occur. At the same time, be honest about what you do and do not know right now. You know that this must occur. You do not yet know *how* the organization will get there. So this story must not commit to any timing, cost, or specific detailed activities. Those will emerge in our second story, and we'll discuss how to get there soon. But right now, do you believe transformation must occur? Are you equipped to start building belief in others, from whom you will need the support to pull it off?

The goal of the Vision Story is to build belief in the need to transform.

A well-executed Vision Story will not only build belief in the need for change, but will also begin building support and setting expectations for later investment in that change. This support will prove valuable at the end of the next phase of our journey, where you will compose the next evolution of your epic tale and seek commitment to begin a Transformation Program.

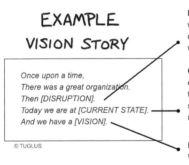

EXAMPLE
VISION STORY

Once upon a time,
There was a great organization.
Then [DISRUPTION].
Today we are at [CURRENT STATE].
And we have a [VISION].

© TUGLUS

Disruption: Our former parent company, whose branded products we still sell, has set out to build a new set of competing products, with a new supplier.

Current State: We have a limited time to continue selling their branded products, and use the current processes and systems for sales and service. This product line accounts for the majority of our division's revenue.

High-Level Vision:
We will develop and launch a new product line, with a new brand and customer-facing experience, that will successfully replace this product line.

Keep moving, there's no time to slow down. It is imperative that you continue telling the Vision Story as we begin the next phase of work. But first, take a moment to feel good about your progress. But only a moment. What you have right now? It's a great start to your epic tale and your transformation, but it is only a start. We need more. This story is still not *real*. If you brought this story to me and asked me to commit to a full-blown Transformation Program, I could not. It's not enough. What exactly am I committing to? What does the future state really look like and what actions are we taking? Can you confidently quantify it in resources and costs, and convey tangible activities that will be undertaken? You cannot. Not yet. We need to make this real. A Reconnaissance Mission is in order.

3
Reconnaissance
Bridging Concept to Reality

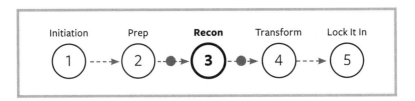

Initiation	Prep	**Recon**	Transform	Lock It In
(1)	(2)	(**3**)	(4)	(5)

IT IS TIME to conduct the Reconnaissance Mission. This is phase 3 of the transformation journey and not to be missed. In order to proceed successfully from here, some very important intel must be acquired. It is imperative that we acquire a better understanding of the future state—and the path to get there—before rushing ahead. As of now, these two elements remain largely unknown, and we need to rectify that.

The Reconnaissance Mission explores how your organization can get from the current state to your vision. The Recon team that you assemble defines the way forward in just the right amount of detail: enough to secure commitment to an actual Transformation Program and to envision a rough roadmap for executing it. This sounds straightforward, but it is trickier than it first appears. Especially with a couple massive pitfalls lurking nearby.

Why is this phase so tricky? Well, you cannot actually get to the vision from the current state (though people will try). Not directly, anyway. Let's look at a real-life business transformation vision to expose this challenge more clearly. Consider the following current state situation and vision, which we first saw in the Vision Story example (see page 91).

THE CHALLENGE: HOW TO GET THERE

CURRENT STATE SITUATION

Your largest insurance product line accounts for the majority of your division's current revenue. In four years, you will lose the rights to sell this product set, and also the ability to use the systems you currently use to sell and service it.

HIGH-LEVEL VISION

Develop and launch a new product line, with a new brand and customer-facing experience, that will successfully replace the product line accounting for the majority of your division's current revenue.

I faced this very challenge. Put yourself in my shoes and imagine you have been handed this information. How would you take an organization to this high-level vision? At first glance, it seems doable: "Let's just jump over there. That cloud looks pretty solid. We'll need some new systems and some branding . . ." But keep thinking about it. Try to imagine the specific activities you will actually need to accomplish. How you would describe them to an execution team? How you will ensure the activities meet the business goals? At this point, in all likelihood, you will find yourself struck by the following thought: "Wait a minute, what precisely *are* the business goals?"

It occurs to you that "customer-facing experience" is not well defined. Nor is "product line." And, now that you think about it, how *would* that future product be sold and serviced? Suddenly you have so many questions: Is the customer experience digital? Must the new product be the same type of product as the one replaced? What about profit margins? The more you think about it, the more certain you become that if you launch yourself at that vision, you will fall straight through.

And you would be right. It is not quite clear what this future world looks like. The vision is lacking substance, missing critical detail. A vision always does. Visions are high-level, strategic concepts. They are not clearly defined models of the future state. And when you haven't defined the future state, how can you possibly map a route— or ask anyone else to map a route—to get there?

NOT ENOUGH INFORMATION TO CHART A JOURNEY

The future state is one of two great unknowns that must be explored before we can begin the actual transformation of an organization. Our high-level vision must be taken and refined into a tangible description of the future state, one with enough clarity that achievement can be measured and a roadmap can be built. The second unknown is that very roadmap. It defines the activities that must be undertaken to get to the future state. To complicate things even further, the current state, analyzed during the Preparation phase, may also require additional clarity. Do not be surprised if it does. That is common, and additional validation of the current state will occur naturally as the other two unknowns are defined.

Once you realize how much work needs to be done, the road ahead can be daunting. Unknowns generate fear, and this is a *lot* of unknown. But you're coming off of a successful Preparation phase, and you believe that transformation is vital. You're doing this. So let's do it right. Without the right experience or guidance, at this precise juncture you may find yourself plunging off a cliff into a potentially fatal pitfall. Carefully step over to the edge to join me for a peek below. You will want to study this one closely.

Pitfall Advisory #5: Too Deep, Too Soon

When you're bolstered by a compelling Vision Story and confident in the need to transform, it is natural to experience a burning desire to dive right into a Transformation Program. After all, the vision appears to be *right there*. And so the order is given: "It's right in front of us. Just run straight ahead. We've got this." Everyone scrambles to move fast. They rush to pull in people from across the company. Initiate deep dives into detailed technology requirements. Hire vendors. Hire consultants. Set up committees. Build a big program management office. Hold huge meetings. There is a flurry of activity.

The intent is great. The energy is amazing. And then they run... right... off... this... cliff and plummet into a common pitfall, where they continue to delve into details, going deep into all variety of detail, until one day they realize they are stuck. They look around, surprised to find they are surrounded by steep walls, and don't know how to get out.

They went too deep, too soon. Attempting to run directly from the current state to the high-level vision is a recipe for disaster. It simply is not feasible. Attempts result in pain, confusion, outsized spending, and a high likelihood of failure. Six to nine months in, these organizations wonder why their transformation effort feels unfocused and out of control, why it takes so long to produce a clear plan, and why it is spending so much, so soon. Twelve to eighteen months later, they wonder why they had to double the budget, and if they should keep going.

Smaller transformations are even more susceptible to getting in too deep, too soon. Easier to comprehend, they can appear deceptively simple and fool you into thinking you can jump right into implementation. But when a nine-month timeline becomes twelve months, then expands to eighteen, there is a good chance you are stuck in this pitfall.

I cannot emphasize enough how common and extremely dangerous this pitfall is. If you find yourself down there and recognize it quickly, it is possible to perform an extraction with relative ease. Consider the following scenario: As part of a larger redesign effort, a team rushes into building new software to replace the current software running their manufacturing plant. Two months in, they realize their future state goals were not well defined and are finding it difficult to connect this software development work to specific, tangible business value. And it is not the only work in the program disconnected from clear business goals. They halt the work, admit the organization moved too quickly, climb out of the pit, and step back to get better future state clarity. They lost a few months and the associated cost, but they have recovered. Not too bad. Lesson learned. It could be much, much worse.

The longer you are in this pit, the harder it is to escape and refocus your initiative. Suppose this same team had spent nine months working on the software, instead of two. They're building that software, defining new processes, and engaging many, many people in many meetings for nine entire months. And *then* they realize that future state goals and value achievement are not well-defined. Now what? Many leaders in this scenario are either not brave enough—or not experienced enough—to step back to assess and adjust. They worry about losing face. They want to avoid exposing the failure, to postpone admitting the financial impact. They may be hoping fervently that it will resolve itself, without drastic intervention. In order to resolve the situation, many leaders will attempt to apply quick fixes to the work in motion. This often leads to a spiraling recurrence of quick fix attempts, all intended to right the ship without drawing attention to the calamity, while in reality pushing it further and further off course.

Do not mistake activity for progress.

What if it were not nine months, but fourteen months, or eighteen months, that had passed before they faced this realization? How hard is it *then* to admit you are stuck in a pit? It only worsens with time. This insidious pitfall will not kill you immediately, but will rather subject you to a slow and painful death. Over time, the transformation will gradually run out of resources and starve, failing to deliver business value as the team runs out of energy and funding.

Unfortunately, many never realize how they got there. Inexperienced leaders are especially susceptible, while well-intended executive sponsors stand by and watch, only to wonder what went wrong. This pitfall can be perplexing to those trapped within it, especially in the beginning, because so much activity is going on. There is so much happening—you must be making progress, right? Do not mistake activity for progress. It is impossible to head directly from your current state to your vision. This is where the Reconnaissance Mission comes in.

> **The goal of transformation is not to get to the program and get it over with. The goal is to get to the business value, as quickly and surely as possible.**

Why You Can't Skip Recon

What business benefits can be realistically expected from your transformation? What activities must occur in order to achieve them? It is important to know what the future state looks like, how much it will cost, and how long it will take. It is critical to define what it is you are really committing to and what it will take to get there. And this all must be done without getting sucked in too deep, too soon.

There are so many unknowns. No worries. That is why you're here. This is perfectly normal. I have been handed some extremely high-level transformation visions, such as the vision I shared earlier to replace a major product line. Sometimes I was provided just a single sentence, like the time I was asked to "figure out what to do about personal data protection and privacy" across a large global company. As is typical of a vision, these did not provide much tangible information about the future state—certainly nowhere near enough information to build a detailed execution plan. But this is to be expected. A transformation journey must begin somewhere. And at the beginning, there is always a looming chasm of unknowns covered by a deep fog, obscuring the route to the other side. Do not let it intimidate you. It is time to dispel that fog that masks the future and map the route.

Recon is powerful, but often skipped or misunderstood. An effective Reconnaissance Mission is one of the most powerful secrets to a successful transformation. Executed well, it provides the critical foundation for the remainder of the transformation journey, offering invaluable clarity regarding the Transformation Program to follow. This clarity enables an executive team to confidently commit to the program and enables a Transformation team to confidently begin the program.

When Reconnaissance is skipped, it is often simply due to a lack of transformation know-how. To the uneducated, it can appear that a transformation consists exclusively of the Transformation Program, because that is where the future state is built. This is a dangerous belief that drives organizations to ignore Initiation, conduct a cursory Preparation phase, and then jump straight into a Transformation Program, after which the journey is deemed complete. Initiatives like this, that skip phases 1, 3, and 5 of the transformation journey, are destined not to achieve real business value. They end up too deep, too soon, and their vision is often impaired by pitfalls as well. You know better than that. The goal of transformation is not to get to the program and get it over with. The goal is to get to the business value, as quickly and surely as possible. Which requires Recon.

Because the Reconnaissance phase is so critical and often misunderstood, let's spend some time laying out the key elements of a good Recon Mission, and look at some examples to help you imagine yours.

Recon is where high-level concepts gain definition and begin to look possible, and possibilities are shaped into something people can believe is achievable.

The Recon Framework

It's mission time. Recon is where high-level concepts gain definition and begin to look possible, and possibilities are shaped into something people can believe is achievable. This is where the foundation is laid for a future that people can envision and work toward.

HIGH LEVEL   MID-LEVEL   DETAILED

VISION → RECON → TRANSFORMATION PROGRAM

RECON

The goal of the Recon Mission is not to get into every detail of every component of the transformation. The goal is to produce a mid-level definition of the transformation journey and the future state, as comprehensively as possible. This is the bridge between the high-level vision and the detailed transformation effort itself, and is critical for three reasons. First, it makes the transformation appear possible, enabling the organization to imagine the way forward. Second, it instills confidence—enough confidence for you to commit to embarking upon a detailed Transformation Program. Third, it provides a starter map: it sets out a skeleton roadmap that equips the future Transformation team to build a program.

ESTIMATION AND CONFIDENCE LEVEL IN THE RECON MISSION

The Recon Mission is all about gaining just the right amount of clarity, so it's important to recognize the significant amount of estimation involved. By the end, the team should feel confident that they have defined all of the components of the future state—in other words, everything that must exist, or come to pass, in order to realize the business value desired by the transformation.

In regard to the activities and resource estimates to achieve these components, the "how" of achieving that future state, you are seeking accuracy, not precision. There are diminishing returns if an attempt is made to get perfect information. Recon does not have enough time for that. Do not forget, the world is moving forward, and your organizational attention span is short. Time is of the essence. When estimating the "how," the team should not be aiming for perfection. Target 90 percent confidence in the output, and do not press the team to be "100 percent confident." (Or worse, something technically impossible, such as "110 percent"—there is no such thing, people!) As the transformation leader or sponsor, you must expect that a few activities will be missed and underestimated. But in a relatively short time period, you can get the future state solidified and the vast majority of activities defined through a solid Recon Mission.

Recon moves fast, maintains focus, and prepares you to take on the Transformation Program successfully. A Recon Mission requires serious commitment, but any organization is capable of executing one. In the next few pages, we will go through the components of an effective Recon Mission: the team and required executive support, the process, your organization's superpower, and the mission's outputs. Ready for some Recon?

THE RECONNAISSANCE MISSION

The mid-level bridge from a
high-level vision to a detailed transformation program.

TEAM	Mix of internal and external. Do not outsource ownership.	PROCESS	• 1 to 6 months • High urgency • Target 90% confidence

POWER
Identify and activate your superpower.

© TUGLUS

OUTPUTS

- Mid-level definition of future state
- Mid-level definition of activities for achieving future state
- Rough transformation roadmap and timing
- Key dependencies
- Draft resource needs (people, budget, facilities…)

The Recon Team and Required Support

A successful Recon Mission relies on assembling the right team. This intrepid team is heading out on an adventure that will build the foundation for your future, and many of the members will also be needed for the subsequent Transformation Program. The Recon team is a group of top talent, composed of three elements: the transformation leader (as detailed on page 76), experts from inside the organization who know the business, and experienced program management professionals. To staff the necessary business expertise to lead your workstreams, look inside your organization for one full-time, dedicated leader from each business area that will be heavily involved in the transformation envisioned. The transformation leader will define the workstreams and assign ownership of each workstream, heavily correlating to each person's area of expertise.

The Recon team should be relatively small. The exact size depends on the scale and complexity of your transformation, but for a large, complex transformation, it would not be surprising to find six full-time people at the core leading the workstreams, plus four to six full-time business experts, and additional part-time resources as needed. All of those team members should be business-knowledgeable individuals recruited from the inside. In addition to your business experts, recruit two or three experienced program managers. These will most likely come from outside your company. When I can find the talent, I prefer to fill the third program manager role with a high-potential internal candidate.

In a less complex transformation, such as one affecting only a single function, a core team might be as small as one program manager, two workstream leads, and a few experts supporting the program leader.

THE RIGHT INTERNAL EXPERTISE AND CAPABILITY

What type of business expertise does the Recon team need? The specific assigned areas depend on your particular transformation and your unique organizational structure.

You might be engaging business areas such as product, pricing, marketing, branding, manufacturing, and servicing, as well as representation from various regions, divisions, or subsidiaries. In every core area identified, you want top talent who truly understand how the business works. These are individuals who know how all the people, processes, data, and systems interact; how customers interact and transact; how business data flows throughout the organization; and how profit and loss are generated.

Typically, these employees have been with the company for eight to ten years. The perfect candidates are not only expert in their business but also share the following characteristics. They:

- Take ownership

- Collaborate well

- Know they don't have all the answers

- Roll up their sleeves to solve problems

- Have a track record of results

- Are respected by employees as well as their peers

Do not overlook the last item: "are respected by employees as well as their peers." These are the people that others rely upon to know how things work and to get things done.

Building this team with the right people will secure the knowledge, connections, and get-it-done attitude necessary to execute the mission effectively and rapidly. It will also help build crucial commitment as your transformation proceeds into further phases of its journey. One of the benefits of staffing the Recon team with this type of top talent is that they already have the trust and respect of their executives. Because of this trust, those executives are biased toward helping them succeed and will be more likely to support the recon work, committing additional resources as requested by these people and—critically—trusting their output.

This connection is a core dynamic of the people system discussed in the first law of transformation (see page 18). It begins to build executive commitment to the transformation, commitment that will help drive a successful Recon Mission now and sow the seeds of ownership that later will feed into the success of your Transformation Program.

CAN YOU USE CONSULTANTS FOR RECON?

You can outsource work, but you cannot outsource ownership. As discussed in phase 2, this is the one thing you must keep in mind whenever you consider outsourcing something (see page 83). Recon is the most critical time to take this to heart.

Can you use consultants for Recon? No. Absolutely not. I strongly recommend against wholesale outsourcing the recon effort. It's great that you're investing in Recon and not going Too Deep, Too Soon (see page 97). But if you outsource it, you will unwittingly handicap your organization at a critical juncture.

If a consulting firm executes Recon, you will not save time, the output will not be as valuable, and critically, you will not build any organizational ownership. Recon is where you begin to build ownership for your transformation. Outsourcing Recon effectively tries to outsource ownership, a calamitous decision leading you directly into a potentially fatal pitfall.

Step right up to this ledge and check out what happens when an organization falls into a pit of outsourcing ownership.

Pitfall Advisory #6: Outsourcing Ownership

You need the intel that Recon can provide. And you know it. But executives don't want to commit the right staff, and some of your favorite consultant pals are making it sound so easy to outsource. Hey, lots of other organizations do it. (You know how I feel about that—don't get me started.) And so you decide to outsource Recon.

Do you feel that wind suddenly rushing past? That would be you plummeting into this pit. Here is what happens now: This immediately signals to the rest of the executive team that the CEO and executive sponsor are not taking this transformation seriously. That this is not critical enough for expert staff to be allocated, so it clearly does not rank highly in importance. Meanwhile, it signals to the broader employee population that an outsider's view will be imposed upon them. If expert staff members are not being engaged and consulted, then how could this plan possibly understand them and their unique strengths?

People—both leadership and the broader employee base—are already being primed to dislike the output. To fear and question the validity of it. And their concern is justified. In the short period during which Recon is conducted, a consulting team will never understand your business as well as your expert talent. Time will be spent teaching consultants, time that could instead be used to build a quality roadmap.

But more important, however, is the issue of ownership. You need organizational buy-in and ownership. Remember our chat about commitment? Ownership is like commitment, but even more powerful. You will not get ownership by sending in consultants. You may even trigger a negative reaction, both to the activity itself and to its outputs. Executives and leaders have no skin in the game. No personal feeling of commitment or ownership. None of them had to supply resources or truly engage in the effort. Why would any of them sign up for the goals and activities created by outsiders?

But if—instead—you staff the Recon team with employees, employees who come from the very areas to be transformed? Well then, now you're building ownership. Now those areas have a personal connection to the work. They have a familiar face that employees know understands their business and challenges. And executives want these people to succeed. This linkage will maintain commitment and begin to create the ownership that you desperately need during your Transformation Program.

There is a greater strategy here, lurking within my methodology, that is important to understand right now: many of the employees active in leading Recon will become critical leaders for the Transformation Program to follow. However, if you outsource Recon, you will have no ownership, *and* you will have no staff ready to jump into a Transformation Program. This will significantly hamper your speed to ramp up such a program and your ability to execute on a true understanding of what has been learned through Recon. This will be further discussed later, during the Transformation Program.

You might say, "I don't have a commitment issue, I just don't think we know how to do this." Perhaps you feel drawn to hire consultants not because of a reticence to staff the right talent, but rather because you are concerned about your organization's lack of know-how. I hear you. It's great that you acknowledge that. But if consultants are necessary, they should be applied sparingly and carefully, in conjunction with the right internal resources. Bring in an experienced senior transformation expert as an advisor. Just a couple days a week can provide the coaching and guidance to help you through that and other challenges.

And remember, you should be hiring an experienced transformation leader and program managers from the outside. You'll need them for the rest of the transformation journey anyway. If, for some reason, you are not hiring them as direct employees, be sure to secure them for the entirety of both the Recon Mission and the subsequent Transformation Program.

No matter how great the consultants' plan is, or how comfortable they may make you feel (thus deceptively reducing your fear), the very act of using them for this critical endeavor will activate the full defensive mechanisms of the people system. Your people will have been biased against taking the suggested transformation journey before you even unveil it to them. Transformation is all about influencing the people system, applying know-how, and building commitment in order to deliver business value. You need to build commitment and ownership for the future. Attempting to outsource ownership is counterproductive. You will be crippling yourself. Do not outsource Recon.

GETTING THE INTERNAL TALENT YOU NEED

In most corporate cultures, forcing top talent onto a new initiative under another leader will generate some drama and political maneuvering. Be ready, and get the best talent you can. It will pay off later. Remember, this is your organization's future.

In a perfect, highly efficient world, the CEO or president will dictate that the right type of talent must be supplied. When your need to transform is compelling enough that it is taken seriously from the top and given significant priority, then this will happen. Some of you have never seen this, but I promise, it does happen.

Often, however, it does not. Sometimes the transformation, though very important, is not treated as absolutely critical and, therefore, not assigned top priority. Sometimes you find yourself living in a corporate culture where top leaders are unwilling to unequivocally support your transformation, even when your business model is losing relevance or a crisis is brewing. There is a complex mix of psychology, politics, and incentives hidden behind that, which, though fascinating, is not why we are here. For now, we will just note that it does happen, and that you may be in that situation.

Regardless of the reason, you as the sponsor or leader of the transformation must negotiate with leaders across the organization for the necessary talent. You have three primary methods at your disposal by which to achieve this:

Vision Story: Use your Vision Story to talk about what's in it for the organization. Appeal to leaders' sense of community and organizational pride. Everyone wants to be part of a great organization: "We have a great foundation, but the world is changing and there is a powerful future to be achieved. It requires the commitment and collaboration of all of us. Everyone's help is needed to put the right people on this to insure the future." As soon as you gain commitment from some leaders, add that to the story for others: "Customer service, logistics, and our Asia-Pacific division have already committed top talent to this initiative. I'm sure you have some outstanding people who could step up to be part of this amazing team . . ."

Opportunities for employees: Highlight what's in it for the employees. It can be hard to find great assignments to develop top talent. This is an amazing opportunity for top talent to stretch themselves, develop their cross-functional collaboration skills, and have a real impact on the organization. Emphasize what a great development opportunity this offers those employees.

Human resources: Human resources knows where the talent is hiding, and they have an incentive both to make this transformation successful and to develop top talent across the enterprise. Partner with them to influence the situation.

Getting the right talent, right now, has far-reaching implications. After the Recon Mission is complete and the commitment is made to move forward, the next phase of the journey is the Transformation Program. When you take the Recon Mission seriously and assemble the right team, as previously mentioned, many of these individuals will be well-positioned for leadership roles on that program team. With the talent already on hand and in the know, your Transformation Program can be rapidly set up and put in motion.

WAIT! I DON'T HAVE MY TRANSFORMATION LEADER ON BOARD YET!

If you are the executive sponsor, in a perfect world, your transformation leader has already been hired and onboarded, or is joining right now as you assemble the Recon team. In reality, you may still be searching for that person. Do not let that stop you from making progress. Start your search, if you have not already done so. Meanwhile, begin identifying the rest of the Recon team talent based on the criteria I just provided, and implement one of two interim solutions for the top leadership position:

1. Find a retired executive or independent consultant with real transformation experience. They should have experience not just sponsoring transformations but actually leading them. Hire them for a nine-month contract to take you through Recon and the subsequent Transformation Program approval process, and to help establish the Transformation Program itself. It is more than worth the investment for the expertise. Even securing a great consultant for 50 percent of their time would be well worth it.

2. Find a leader within your organization that has some of the characteristics of a transformation leader. Free them up to spend at least 75 percent of their time on this. They must be good at fearlessly removing barriers for the team, trusting the team's expertise, and helping them shape a story. And they must feel true ownership for the future of the organization. Support this leader with an experienced transformation executive coach. Target an engagement of 20 percent of the coach's time.

In either scenario, that interim leader will be able to help onboard and educate the transformation leader when they arrive. The individual in option 1 will be especially good at this. If you choose option 2, where your interim leader comes from the inside, do not assume that this leader can also handle the Transformation Program to follow. That is an entirely different ball game and far more complex. Review the characteristics of a great transformation leader (see page 78), get counsel from the coach, and assess the interim leader's capabilities carefully.

SUPPORTING THE RECON TEAM

Executives must support the urgency of the Recon Mission. This team is operating within a tight time frame, with serious business implications on the line. While building the Recon team, set up their executive support system.

It is the responsibility of the executive sponsor and the transformation leader to gain executive leadership commitment to the mission-critical nature of this activity. The entire leadership team of your organization must understand that Recon is intense work executed under a tight deadline. This is where the Vision Story comes in handy again. Use it often in your conversations to gain support.

The Recon team must be granted the authority and autonomy to define the future of their organization, and their requests must be treated with priority. Speaking of requests, the first request from the team will be any additional experts they need, from across the organization, in order to effectively execute their mission. They will also need dedicated meeting space, and a travel and expense budget that reflects both the need for urgency and the degree to which the business is geographically distributed. Once you have assembled the team and secured the right support, set the time length for Recon and give them their mission orders.

CHOOSING THE LENGTH OF TIME FOR RECON

Set a firm time length for the Recon phase. Recon, by its very nature, has a strong sense of urgency. A mission can range anywhere from one to six months in length, depending on your unique situation. What is important here is that you commit to a specific length of time and hold firm to it. Not everyone is repositioning a Fortune 50 company or replacing the entire global manufacturing platform in a heavily distributed organization. If this does sound like your situation, set the length of your Recon Mission at the higher end, at four to six months. Running a relatively low complexity transformation? Do not skip Recon! Give yourself a solid month or two. That pitfall is lurking nearby. You know the one. You don't want to suddenly find yourself too deep, too soon.

THE MISSION

Good morning, team.

Your mission, should you choose to accept it, is a mission of reconnaissance. You must discover what it will take to execute a complete transformation of your business. You have been provided three files:

· *Details of industry unrest and disruption that threaten this very organization.*

· *A surveillance report of our current situation. It should be complete, but verify as necessary.*

· *What little intel we have regarding our target, the future transformed state of the organization. There is a high-level vision contained within the Vision Story.*

This is a top priority for us. Act with extreme urgency.

Identify the key transformation activities and expose major dependencies. Deliver a validation of the current state, a refined future state, and the transformation architecture and roadmap. Included in your report must be assumptions and estimates for required resources, including time and cost. Be sure to take into account the laws of transformation. Although time is limited, accuracy (but not precision) is crucial. You must be at least 90 percent confident in the accuracy of all the intel and recommendations included in your report. And you must be especially confident that you have identified all future state components.

Note that your team has been assembled for you. You will choose any additional agents to be engaged. You have three months to complete your mission. Work closely as a team—you will need all of your skills, contacts, and knowledge to succeed.

The future of the organization is in your hands . . .

Good luck, team.

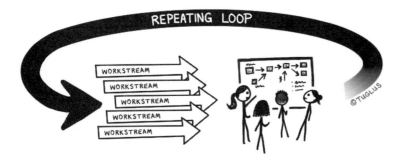

The Recon Process

Now that the team has been assembled and received their mission orders, it is time to leap into action. If you are the executive sponsor and have hired a great leader, you may choose to skip the next few pages regarding the Recon process and pick up again where I discuss the role of the Transformation leader in Recon (on page 121). For everyone else, let's run through how to run an effective Recon Mission.

This is a business-driven, highly collaborative, fast-moving process that engages in adaptive planning and develops the outputs in an evolutionary manner. Sound complicated? It's not. Let's get into it.

First, the team must move fast. Workstreams should spend no more than a few days roughing out a plan and brainstorming initial areas to pursue before they kick into high gear. From there on out, it should be all about iterating to define the future state and determining the activities that will form the bridge to get there. On a weekly basis, bring all workstream leads together to collaboratively map connections and uncover assumptions and dependencies.

RECON IN ACTION: AN EXAMPLE

To help you imagine a Recon Mission, let's build on the vision shared earlier in the chapter (see page 94). As you can see in the following graphic, I identified five workstreams and assigned a leader to each. To give you a flavor of what happened, we'll focus in on the activity of just one workstream, the Brand & Marketing workstream.

VISION

Develop and launch a new product line, with a **new brand** and customer-facing experience, that will successfully replace a product line accounting for the majority of the division's current revenue

WORKSTREAMS

Brand & Marketing

Product & Pricing

Contracts & Sales

Servicing & Operations

Financial Ops & Collections

Looking at the vision statement, you can see that the Brand & Marketing workstream had a two-word high-level vision—"new brand"— that was not terribly descriptive (as can be expected). Through Recon, the workstream team iteratively decomposed that into more and more pieces to get to a mid-level definition of the future state of "new brand." The team iteratively researched and assessed the activities that would need to be executed, generating and evaluating options for execution, and making decisions.

You can see from the diagram below that their mid-level future state included the following: there would be a new brand name; it would fit with the existing branding across the corporation; and it would have a logo, a color palette, brochures, and ad campaigns. It would also need staff for marketing and brand management. For each activity identified, the team also estimated resources, cost, and the amount of time that would be required for execution.

Ultimately, the team produced a clear, mid-level future state for "new brand" and a solid understanding of the activities required to achieve it. To do this, they had to think through how those would be executed, without going too deep. It is important to understand that the team did not create step-by-step plans for how to conduct any of the activities. Nor did they evaluate and choose any vendors that would execute the activities. They *did* look at past work for a sense of scale and complexity, and they contacted colleagues and experts who had executed similar work in order to inform the rough estimates that they created. But they avoided going too deep and held firm to developing just enough detail to be confident that they had identified all the components of the future state and were accurate—but not precise—in identifying all the activities and estimating the effort.

HIGH-LEVEL

NEW BRAND

MID-LEVEL

©TuGLuS

FUTURE STATE	ACTIVITIES	👥	💲	RESOURCE NOTES	TIME	DEPENDENCIES & ASSUMPTIONS
• BRAND NAME	• BRAND RESEARCH	#	$	～～～	# MONTHS	• BRAND NAME READY FOR FORMS FILING 3 MONTHS PRIOR TO STATE APPROVAL
• FITS W/ EXISTING BRANDS	• BRAND DECISION	#	$	～～～	# WEEKS	
• BRAND USAGE DEFINED	• TRADEMARK SEARCH	#	$	～～～	# WEEKS	
• LOGO	• DESIGN & EXECUTE LAUNCH CAMPAIGN	#	$	～～～	# MONTHS	• ～～～ ～～～
• COLOR PALETTE						
• BROCHURES	• LOGO/DESIGN CREATION	#	$	～～	# MONTHS	• ～～ ～～
• AD CAMPAIGNS						
• MARKETING 👥	• BROCHURE DESIGN	#	$	～～～	# WEEKS	
• BRAND MGMT 🧍	• ～～～～	#	$	～～～	～～	• ～～ ～～
• ～～～～	• ～～～～	#	$	～～～	～～	

This undertaking may seem simple, based on the example, but it requires a true understanding of how the business operates today. This is why you need the right internal talent involved. Assumptions about the current state are regularly found to be inaccurate under the scrutiny of a Recon Mission, and accuracy can be essential, especially when contemplating alterations to data, systems, or machinery. Throughout the mission, Recon teams will regularly reveal new information that leads to adjustments in previously defined future state components, activities, or estimates. The greatest complexity, however, comes not from getting the clarity for individual activities, but from the interconnections between activities and across workstreams. In other words, identifying major dependencies.

DEPENDENCIES MUST BE EXPOSED

Dependencies, undiscovered, can lead to significant unexpected delays and overruns during your future Transformation Program. And they can be deviously difficult to unveil. The trickiest ones to uncover are those that cut across workstreams to connect seemingly independent activities. Or connect to external activities, those outside of the transformation's territory.

For example, a very common external dependency manifests when an operating platform replacement is in motion somewhere else in the corporation, running concurrently. Your transformation assumes you will launch your products on the new platform. There are things you would do differently if you instead assumed you would launch on the current platform. Your Transformation team must recognize that there exists a dependency here. That the success of your plans is dependent upon this executing as advertised. It must recognize that (A) this platform project is happening, (B) it is relevant to your transformation, and (C) it could have a meaningful impact on your transformation if, for some reason, it does not deliver as expected.

With this situation noted, savvy transformation leadership will later devise a Plan B in case the new platform is not ready when they need it—but later, not now. They will not create Plan B now, during Recon, but will do so during the Transformation Program. Right now, they just need to recognize the dependency, note it, and communicate it to set expectations. You might be thinking "these sound like risks." You'd be right. The dependencies outside of your control are risks, risks that really matter—not the kind that reside in a risk cauldron. It doesn't matter whether you track them as "risks," key dependencies, or assumptions. What matters is that you identify them now, and actively monitor and protect against them during the Transformation Program ahead.

As workstream leads come together weekly to compare notes and inform each other's work, their focus should be on uncovering these dependencies. Successfully mapping these—both among activities within the transformation, and between transformation activities and activities external to this transformation—is essential in order to lay out a reliable roadmap, time estimate, and cost estimate.

It is easy to miss the importance of this. Many assume that it will naturally happen, or that just one or two short sessions will handle it. That would be unwise. Regular conversations about dependencies must be conducted. Weekly is good. It only takes a single missed dependency to lead to months of delay, adding unanticipated additional time and cost to your Transformation Program.

To envision this more clearly, let's revisit that Brand & Marketing workstream, during a time when a major dependency was uncovered.

The Brand workstream was iterating along happily. Meanwhile, the Product & Pricing workstream was operating in parallel, also identifying activities to bridge the current state to the future state. Unbeknownst to Brand, Product identified an activity of particular relevance to them: the new product and pricing must be filed with each state prior to launch. At first glance, it is not obvious why Brand should care.

However, the new brand name needed to be included within that filing. And this created a dependency: the brand name would need to be finalized well in advance of the date those product forms would be submitted for state approval. This dependency did not naturally become clear while the two workstreams worked independently. The Product workstream was assuming, without really thinking about it, that the brand name would be available for the forms to be filed. The Brand workstream was only thinking the name needed to be completed in advance of finalizing marketing materials and ad campaigns—they knew nothing about product filing.

Sometimes dependencies will be identified organically, based on the experience and relationships of the individuals involved. The more knowledgeable the team members are about how the business works, the more likely they are to see these dependencies or discover them in the normal course of conversation with colleagues. But we cannot rely upon that. So how are they identified? Who makes this connection between workstreams? This is where those program managers and that transformation leader really shine. Let's visit one of the weekly all-workstream collaboration meetings to see this in action.

Product workstream lead: One of the activities we defined this week was filing the product with the state regulators.

Program manager: What needs to be included in the filing? How long does it take to file?

Product workstream lead: It depends on the state or province. Could take two days or two months. The product forms must be filed. They'll need product name, pricing, maybe some feature information.

Program manager: What is the longest and most onerous set of state requirements? Product and Brand teams, take note: it looks like we have an important dependency here. Right after this meeting, let's get together to make sure we understand it and log it.

After further discussion, it was decided that the brand name and pricing needed to be completed three months in advance of launch, to allow for review time and to buffer for any potential delays or back-and-forth with the state regulators. Had this dependency not been brought to light, the Brand team would have planned to have the name finalized much closer to launch, thinking only to have it ready for the marketing materials a month prior to launch.

This example depicts how dependencies are brought to light and handled. It also demonstrates how just one dependency, had it gone unidentified, could later have resulted in a two-month delay in the Transformation Program. A good Reconnaissance Mission will investigate and uncover many of these. Any workstream lead may identify dependencies, but most often it is the program managers or transformation leader who will see them.

This example also highlights why it is so important to have the right composition of internal and external talent on the Recon team (see page 103). Internal talent is placed on the team because they are connected to the business today and know how the business really works. External expertise in transformation leadership is placed on the team because they know how to pull together a transformation.

In any organization, there will naturally be gaps and gray zones between business areas. Program managers are there to identify the gaps and potential connections that naturally appear between business areas, and drive cross-functional exploration into those spaces. They continuously scan for dependencies. It was a program manager who saw the filing dependency for what it was—a vital connection point within the transformation.

Program managers are also responsible for ensuring the mission executes quickly and comprehensively. They keep an eye on the clock and rely on experience to strike the right balance between details and speed. They know when to initiate a deeper analysis and where activities hold the greatest potential for material surprises, long lead times, or especially complex interdependencies. If they feel that people have not gone deep enough in an area, they will push the team to go further. Getting too deep? Program managers will pull them out of the weeds.

There is an art to knowing the right amount of depth. This is a place where experienced program leadership really pays off. Inexperienced or weak program leaders will not recognize where to go into more or less detail. They will put the mission at risk—and ultimately your Transformation Program as well—by conducting cursory overviews, overlooking dependencies, and pursuing perfect information.

THE ROLE OF THE TRANSFORMATION LEADER IN RECON

The transformation leader is accountable for the outputs of the Recon Mission and must be actively engaged in the process. And I will emphasize this: *active engagement is mandatory.* I have seen inexperienced executive-level leaders try to lead a transformation with a hands-off approach. It does not work. This is a high-stakes,

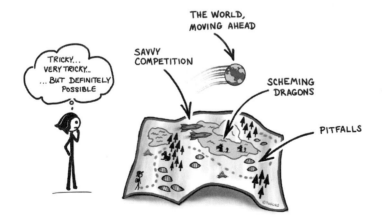

high-complexity, urgent operation, and it is way too critical for passive leadership.

To avoid misinterpretation, let's be explicit: I do not mean micromanagement. Not at all. What I mean is that the transformation leader has a distinct and active role to play. They must keep an eye on the big picture, shape the story, steer the team around pitfalls, watch for unnoticed dependencies, and manage expectations across the enterprise. They will also create the draft of an organizational chart for the Transformation Program, with roles and responsibilities, and include this in the Recon output. If a transformation leader is to effectively play their role, they must be actively engaged.

The transformation leader spends much of their time with the workstream leads: listening to findings, watching for gaps, considering assumptions and dependencies, and drawing attention to looming pitfalls. They also have the experience to gut check and adjust estimates. They know where additional risks may be lurking.

Intently focused on taking the organization forward and driving real business value, the transformation leader is always working on three things during Recon. First, they are setting up for that transformation ahead: Telling the Vision Story, setting expectations, and beginning to envision the creation and setup of the Transformation Program. A large portion of their time is spent managing expectations of business area executives across the enterprise, helping them understand what is coming and the role they will play. Second, they are beginning to shape the next big evolution of their epic tale: a strong, solid story—a real story—that gains commitment and lays out the roadmap for the transformation to follow. Third, they are strategizing around how best to take the broader organization on this transformation journey—how to connect with employees, engage them, and dispel fear.

HOW'S THAT VISION STORY GOING?

While conducting Recon, you have in parallel been sharing your Vision Story with key leaders (see page 89), spreading your powerful belief in the need to transform.

Ironically, as that succeeds and belief begins to build across the executive team, fear builds as well, one of the very forces that makes transformation so difficult. Savvy transformation leaders know that as they share their story, inspiring and growing belief in the need to change, they are simultaneously drawing attention to the fact that big changes must occur, signaling that great unknowns lie ahead. And unknowns, of course, generate fear.

You will be tackling that fear shortly, but right now this is the reality: The future state is largely unknown. Because of this, it is critical to share the Vision Story repetitively and consistently to build more familiarity and comfort with the notion. Share it regularly with the leaders from whom you need commitment and support—executives, board members, other key leaders as applicable. When people become genuinely engaged in the possibilities conveyed by your vision, they will want to know details. Things like timing, cost, and activities will be requested. This is a good sign, and you can confidently inform them that while you do not currently have those answers, you will by a specific date—the date the Reconnaissance Mission is completed. That is when you will be ready to share your Transformation Story, which includes those answers.

Superpower Activation

There is something special about your business. If you identify it and put it at the heart of your transformation, you will dramatically improve your ability to take people on the journey with you. What is your organization's core purpose? What do you stand for? What is the unique glue that underpins your organization's existence? I am talking about your sustainable superpower, the irrefutable core strength and purpose

The Vision Story inspires, but also introduces fear.

that will remain at the heart of your company well into the future. Walmart's lies within its obsession of saving customers money through low prices. Patagonia's manifests in its love of the outdoors. What's yours?

Part of the transformation leader's job during Recon is not only to figure out what will change in the future, but also what will not change. More precisely, it's the leader's job to identify the existing core beliefs or shared purpose that will hold true in the future state. Once identified, this will be used to engage employees in the transformation journey and dispel fear. During Recon is the time to activate your superpower.

Back in the early 2000s, I was a contractor on a large program at the US Centers for Disease Control and Prevention (CDC). The program to develop a National Electronic Disease Surveillance System (NEDSS, because everything needs an acronym) was established to enable rapid sharing of disease data across the health system. Here's an example: Back in the old days, processes were paper-based and manual. If an epidemic were breaking out, just a case or two at a time across different states, it might not be obvious for months. But with connected systems and common processes, the CDC would be able to identify quickly what was happening and take action immediately. Pretty important, right?

I was hired on to the program as a "principal business process reengineering specialist." Huh? Admit it, that title is so jargonized it would stop anyone in their tracks. No joke, this is what showed up on my business cards. Some of the CDC guys even tried to turn it into an acronym: "Ah, you're a PBPRS." I'm sure they were just messing with me. Well, pretty sure. OK, to be honest, I still wonder.

Anyway, my role was to help the CDC define and document the requirements for the first version of this solution. The program engaged many health professionals, hailing from far and wide across the public health system. I was leading lengthy requirements workshops, often with dozens of people in the room. With their diversity of experience and roles, it was not surprising to discover they also held many differences of opinion. Some people thought they knew all the answers. Others made it clear that they would rather be back at their day jobs. Some very nicely informed me that all this work was not part of their job description. Others not as nicely. Initial meetings devolved into squabbles and slow progress.

Although I was diligently prepared to lead the meetings and guide them through decisions, it was a struggle to keep everyone energized and focused. After a few sessions of this, many hours wracking my brain for a solution, and approaching some attendees individually for advice, it finally hit me. What was needed was to find something they shared in common that could bond them together, something that was more powerful than their differences. I thought back to my start-up experience and how powerful it was to have a shared purpose that energized us to take on the world. Was there something here that would bring these health care professionals together? Something that would continue to hold true throughout this program and into the future?

There was one thing I could identify that everyone in that room stood behind. That played a role in each person's decision to go into their career. That no one could refute. At the heart of this people system was a shared purpose to improve health care. Every single person in that system cared deeply about improving health care. And when they remembered this, they were able to come together to truly engage—with focus—in their transformation.

Once their shared purpose had been identified, I experimented by beginning the next meeting with the following statement: "We are all here today to improve health care. Today we will focus on this aspect..." And then I repeated that phrase at various intervals throughout the day.

Did it change things? Absolutely. Dramatically. It was like I had discovered a switch, that when flipped, transformed boring detail work into purposeful design. I had aligned our meetings to a greater purpose that resonated with this diverse system of people. From then on, I began every meeting that way.

A superpower is a shared purpose that seems obvious once you identify it. When you hear someone say, "our core reason for existence is ..." or "our core shared belief is..." and the full statement seems obvious to you, and eternally true, then you have found one. In the CDC example, once I said that "every single person in that system cared deeply about improving health care," I bet you thought, "Of course. Obviously." That seemed so obvious, right? Easy to keep in mind? Well, it always looks easier from the outside. The thing is, we all need to be reminded of our superpower, because it is easy to lose sight of it. Over time, when we're immersed in the day-to-day, our shared superpower fades out of sight and hides in the back of our minds, waiting to be called to duty.

Your organization's superpower is just lying dormant, waiting to be activated. Properly deployed, it will ground your organization in something familiar as you take people through the upcoming period of great change. It will reduce fear and make them more willing to engage in the journey. Do not underestimate the impact of doing this. This is what connects your transformation to the core culture of the organization. It is the lifeline that connects the current state to the future, through the arduous journey of transformation. Your superpower is a powerful element of the story you are about to tell, and it will become especially important beyond that as well, in the execution and sustainability of your transformation. We will revisit this during those phases of the journey.

There is something about your organization that makes it special. Define it. Treat it with respect. Make sure your team takes it to heart.

Bust out the capes!

ACROSS THE ENTERPRISE...

The Recon Report: The Outputs of the Mission

Recon will be intense and go by quickly. Once the mission is complete, it is time to read the recon report and hear the debrief.

You went into this mission with a high-level vision for the future of your organization, and a lot of uncertainty. Both the future state and how to get there were very much unknown. Some very talented people have worked hard over the past few months to reduce that uncertainty and translate that vision into something more tangible. In addition to your superpower, the output of the Recon team should include the following:

- Mid-level definition of the future state

- Mid-level definition of activities (tactics) for achieving the future state

- Rough transformation roadmap and timing

- Key dependencies

- Draft of resource needs (people, budget, facilities, etc.)

Embedded within this output will be the inclusion of activities or tools to take advantage of disruption opportunities or combat threats. (Remember, disruption can include competitor actions, technologies, new business concepts, and so on.) Also, the team should feel confident in their understanding of the current state, having validated it as they defined the pathway to the future.

The precise activities and future state contained within your own recon report will, of course, depend upon the type of transformation that you set out to explore. It may define new departments or business areas to be built, along with what their success measures would be. It may lay out new channels or new customer experiences for existing products, or it may define altogether new service offerings. It may or may not call out some technologies specifically.

Let's look at an excerpt of an example recon report. Suppose that your transformation is a very operational, productivity-focused endeavor to improve transactional speed and cost. We'll look at the portion of the recon report that addresses the customer ordering process. It could include future state components and activities such as those below:

- **High-level vision:** "Significantly improve speed and cost of customer transactions without negatively impacting the customer closing percentage."

- **Workstream:** The customer ordering process

- **Future state:** The customer ordering process is reduced from 4 minutes to 2 minutes, and the cost per transaction is reduced by 50 percent, from $___ to $___. Components include: a reengineered process with significant automation, new supporting job procedures and role definitions, a new organizational design, new operating metrics, and a revised operating budget. There will also be new digital tools to support this.

- **Activities:**

  - Decompose, assess, and reengineer processes

  - Conduct user experience testing—baseline and multiple phases

  - Choose, procure, and implement automation tools. Note: It is estimated that 80 percent (from 35 percent today) of customer order-to-confirmation can be automated.

  - Redesign and implement new job roles and procedures

- Define, approve, and institute new operating metrics and targets for each subprocess and role

- Define, approve, and institute new operating metrics and targets for technology

- Define and implement any new security or business continuity support

- Negotiate with external support teams and vendors for changes to processes and technology managed by them

- Rewrite and approve vendor contracts

- And more . . .

- **Key dependencies:**

    - Vendor willingness and flexibility in contract negotiation, adopting new processes, and implementing technology changes

    - Website redesign work that is in development concurrently is assumed to be fully complete prior to any testing of the new customer ordering process

    - Divisions under consideration for divestiture are assumed out of scope

- **A rough roadmap and timeline:** These are included and depict a recommended four-phase implementation plan, with numerous concurrent activities. The expected business value that will be achieved at different stages is estimated, including staff reductions and other cost impacts.

- **Draft resource needs:** The cost of the work and tools is estimated at $___ and includes ___ people. Time to implement the new world and immerse the staff will be ___. The required Transformation team composition and structure are also attached.

In this example, the Recon team has provided the future state goal, the estimated cost, and the tactical actions that need to be taken. They have researched the potential for automation and process reengineering, and educated themselves enough on the current state processes to know that a 50 percent reduction in time and cost and 80 percent automation all make sense—that they are both valuable and feasible goals. At the same time, the team has resisted going too deep. They have not chosen specific brands of tools. Nor have they defined precisely all the details of the process changes to be made. They have gone just far enough to feel they can estimate within the necessary margin of confidence.

Let's review another example. There will often be culture-related items in the mission report. Some leaders feel uncomfortable with culture-related goals because they perceive them to be too difficult to measure. Although these can be more qualitative than quantitative, progress of culture change can definitely be assessed. I once set a high-level vision for my organization to achieve a "sustainable culture of innovation." From that, the defined mid-level future state included:

· No one uses "because we've always done it this way" as a blanket justification anymore (the number one current state rationale for not trying something new or seriously considering it).

- A "test and learn" mindset is embedded in all customer-facing operations: at least three tests are in process at all times, and at least ten are executed per year.

- An annual innovation competition is held with training and support provided to all who participate, and multiple concepts brought forward will be pursued further with management support.

As you can see, this mid-level definition of the future state sets out goals that are specific enough to measure. This example also speaks to the diversity of transformation, demonstrating how each unique transformation can look different.

In this situation, I deliberately defined some of the goals to gain further specificity over time. For instance, the third item above says "*multiple* concepts brought forward will be pursued," instead of a specific number. After the first competition, I supported the further development of *any* concept that exhibited a productive combination of management interest and employee enthusiasm. Thus, all concepts that drove the culture of innovation forward (the vision being pursued) received support to proceed. It turned out, after a few competitions, that the right answer, given the goal, was not as clear-cut as a numerical target. We learned that as many as 75 percent of concepts in a year could continue forward, but not in the way we anticipated. Some concepts were similar, and teams joined forces to work together. Some people were excited about continuing to pursue their concept, and others were not. It was revealed that some concepts brought to the competition were already being considered elsewhere in the organization, and this work just energized and bolstered that work. And some concepts attracted strong enough leadership interest that they quickly became official operating projects.

Recon is not about locking in precise numbers. It is about defining real goals that achieve the desired business value. Sometimes that involves numbers, sometimes it does not.

RECON COMBATS SCOPE CREEP

Most people don't think about scope creep—where more and more work is added to a program, ballooning time, cost, and complexity— until later. Until they are in the depths of the Transformation Program itself. But I want you to spend a moment thinking about that now.

Avoiding scope creep is one more reason to take Recon seriously. A proper Reconnaissance Mission will protect against most scope creep by clearly setting out the goals and activities of the program to come. And experienced transformation know-how will handle the rest—a good transformation leader will help the organization identify when increases to scope are necessary and valuable, and guard against those that are not.

If you end up with a runaway scope problem in your program, then you did not conduct a solid Recon, or you have weak transformation leadership. Or both.

Recon delivers the roadmap for transformation. A good Recon Mission will pay for itself many times over with better focus, ownership, and organizational clarity—all of which dramatically increase your chances of a successful transformation. Don't outsource it. Don't minimize it. And absolutely do not skip it.

If you are still contemplating skipping Recon, step back for a moment. Consider that most transformations fail to deliver the intended value. Remember, it is not just that most people do not know what to do. It is also that transformation requires continuous commitment and hard work from the very beginning. If you are not willing to execute a serious Recon Mission, I don't know how you can confidently execute a Transformation Program.

Just how important is this transformation to you? If you're not serious, acknowledge that and move on. Do not set your employees and investors up for disillusionment. Chances are, they know change is needed. Do it or do not. But do not pretend. That is just wasting energy that could be applied elsewhere. Perhaps in selling off your business.

At the end of the day, the Recon Mission provides a mid-level view of the future state and a rough game plan. This is foundational groundwork that a Transformation Program team will be able to use as a starting point. This mission also begins to set expectations and build a fledgling sense of ownership across the executive team and the organization. Through Recon, executives have developed a sense of what is coming and what it will entail.

A good Reconnaissance Mission will pay for itself many times over with better focus, ownership, and organizational clarity.

Thanks to the Reconnaissance Mission, you now possess valuable intel regarding the future and how to achieve it. Look to the future with confidence. *We can do this. We see what needs to be done. We know this is possible.* You are ready to tell your Transformation Story. This critical point in our journey will determine just how serious your organization is.

Transformation Story

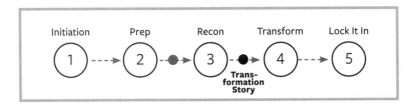

Initiation	Prep	Recon	Transform	Lock It In
1	2	3	4	5

Trans-
formation
Story

THE TRANSFORMATION STORY is the next great evolution of your epic tale, deliberately crafted with one goal in mind: secure commitment to transform. Specifically, commitment from the entire executive team to commission a Transformation Program and to support the urgency and criticality of the program, including the provision of funding and talent.

Even if you are the CEO, you will need commitment and support from others in order to execute a successful Transformation Program. You may be able to unilaterally allot the money and headcount, but you need your executive team to join you on this journey, and you must be able to confidently convey your plan to the board. A transformation cannot be executed alone.

The Transformation Story convinces people that your transformation is not only necessary, but that it is possible.

What makes the Transformation Story so powerful? There is a compelling reason for your business to change, and this story makes it real. It makes it possible. It not only shares *why* the organization must change, as provided by work done in the Preparation phase (see page 53), but it also *makes it real* by describing what the future looks like and how your organization will get there. It communicates that you are ready to begin a Transformation Program to make that future come to life because now you *know what to do.* The Transformation Story convinces people that your transformation is not only necessary, but that *it is possible.* That is the magic of this story.

Let's take a look at the components, using the template below as a guide. Notice that the first part of the Transformation Story is your Vision Story, which inspires belief in the need to transform. This should feel familiar to your audience by now, as you have continued to tell this story throughout the time Recon was conducted. The second part of this story uses the discrete outputs from the Recon phase—an organization's superpower, future state, and specific actions—to make that vision real. To depict a clear future state and demonstrate that it is achievable. Commitment can now be secured for a Transformation Program.

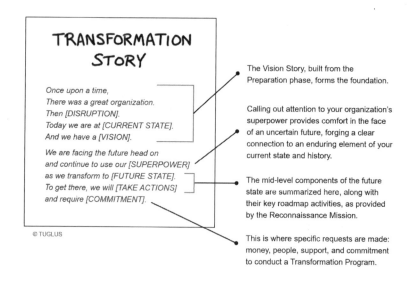

TRANSFORMATION STORY

Once upon a time,
There was a great organization.
Then [DISRUPTION].
Today we are at [CURRENT STATE].
And we have a [VISION].

We are facing the future head on
and continue to use our [SUPERPOWER]
as we transform to [FUTURE STATE].
To get there, we will [TAKE ACTIONS]
and require [COMMITMENT].

© TUGLUS

The Vision Story, built from the Preparation phase, forms the foundation.

Calling out attention to your organization's superpower provides comfort in the face of an uncertain future, forging a clear connection to an enduring element of your current state and history.

The mid-level components of the future state are summarized here, along with their key roadmap activities, as provided by the Reconnaissance Mission.

This is where specific requests are made: money, people, support, and commitment to conduct a Transformation Program.

In most organizations, this story will be presented to a leadership committee for sign-off—potentially multiple committees, depending upon your organization's governance procedures. Fortunately, you have a pretty solid understanding of the road ahead, and you'll be able to confidently discuss this transformation with anyone.

Thanks to Recon, the future is no longer unknown, just not yet achieved.

As you head to this leadership committee meeting, about to request commitment for what may be the most audacious undertaking of your career, you take stock of your situation. You have completed Initiation, Preparation, and the Reconnaissance Mission, and masterfully bypassed all the pitfalls hidden within. Although you have successfully educated everyone here regarding the need to change through the Vision Story, they are, understandably, wary of the unknown future. But you are here to dispel much of that unknown.

Your story today will tell them that, thanks to Recon, the future is no longer unknown. It is just not yet achieved. To encourage shared ownership in this future, you will remind them that some of their best people have been engaged in this transformation. People that they trust. People who know how their business works. Those people, those expert and talented individuals, have both brought clarity to the previously unknown future and found a way to make it possible. You are confident in the story you have crafted and feel well equipped to have the conversation. In fact, you look forward to it.

An example Transformation Story is provided on page 138. As you read through it, consider how best to tell your own unique story. And know that though I start with disruption in my examples, it is not the only way to tell the story. You can begin the story wherever is most effective. If the current state is dire, that can be a powerful story starter, especially if the audience is facing this reality for the first time. It can provide a shocking wake-up call, followed up with a confident plan for the way forward. Starting instead with your superpower, on the other hand, reminds everyone that this is a great business with a shared history and shared purpose. It grounds the audience in the known, in something familiar and irrefutable.

EXAMPLE
TRANSFORMATION STORY

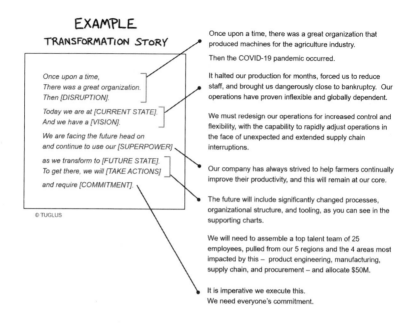

Once upon a time,
There was a great organization.
Then [DISRUPTION].

Today we are at [CURRENT STATE].
And we have a [VISION].

We are facing the future head on
and continue to use our [SUPERPOWER]

as we transform to [FUTURE STATE].
To get there, we will [TAKE ACTIONS]
and require [COMMITMENT].

© TUGLUS

Once upon a time, there was a great organization that produced machines for the agriculture industry.
Then the COVID-19 pandemic occurred.

It halted our production for months, forced us to reduce staff, and brought us dangerously close to bankruptcy. Our operations have proven inflexible and globally dependent.

We must redesign our operations for increased control and flexibility, with the capability to rapidly adjust operations in the face of unexpected and extended supply chain interruptions.

Our company has always strived to help farmers continually improve their productivity, and this will remain at our core.

The future will include significantly changed processes, organizational structure, and tooling, as you can see in the supporting charts.

We will need to assemble a top talent team of 25 employees, pulled from our 5 regions and the 4 areas most impacted by this – product engineering, manufacturing, supply chain, and procurement – and allocate $50M.

It is imperative we execute this.
We need everyone's commitment.

Another option is to first paint the picture of a great future state, which can be inspiring, but is rarely a strong start unless you weave in disruption well. Also, remember the third law, about the power of relativity (see page 34)? The future state, by itself, lacks context. It is more powerful when communicated relative to something else. Disruption can provide a dramatic opening. An attention-grabbing video or a physical demonstration can showcase disruptive forces that will be harnessed. Keep in mind that this story is about making things real, so do not be shy in bringing in virtual and physical demos of technology or processes, of the current state or disruption. Suppose you are talking about improving visibility into your operations, and sensors will be part of that. Bring in some sensors and pass them around to point out just how small and cheap they are as you discuss their potential to create business value, so people can hold them and look at them. Send packages of the demonstration sensors to remote attendees. To demonstrate a relevant process or concept from another industry, show a video or interview clip—or better yet, introduce a person live via video to share how it works there. With real-life examples, your story is more effective because you are making that unknown future more tangible and real.

Depending upon your corporate culture, it may take time for sign-off. But once the official commitment has been made, a sense of urgency will build quickly. Action will be expected. With your Recon work, you are ready to capitalize on this energy to move full steam ahead. Unlike previously, back before Recon—where you risked going too deep, too soon—you are now well prepared to springboard off this enthusiasm and confidently leap into action. You are equipped to move fast, yet with focus. You are prepared to lead the organization forward: "Here is what you can expect next, here is what we need from you, here is where we are going."

However you choose to compose the story, the goal is the same: get commitment. So, are you doing this? Are you serious about transformation? It is time to commit.

THE EPIC TALE EVOLVES AND EXPANDS OVER TIME

Your Transformation team will expand upon and share the Transformation Story in their own words many times, in many places. It will grow and take on life throughout the remainder of the journey. Once you have secured commitment to begin the program, you will want to continue leveraging this story to introduce other people to the transformation journey, to engage them, and to inspire them to join you. Throughout the course of a transformation, I tell versions of this story hundreds of times. It can be organized many ways, with detail added where needed, and structured for maximum impact based on the audience.

Each time you tell the story, carefully consider where the audience lies in terms of understanding, expectations, and commitment, and always keep in mind that attention spans are short and getting shorter. Based on that, craft the order of the pieces and choose how much detail and time to devote to each one.

It is time to transform. The future now appears both compelling and possible. The Transformation Story has been told. It achieves the desired effect: Commitment has been secured. It's a "go." You are cleared to set up a Transformation Program. Grab your gear and get moving. There is no time to waste.

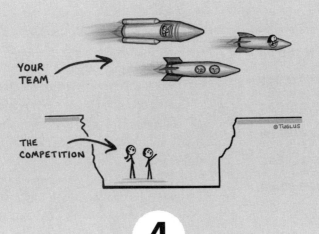

4
Transformation Program
Constructing the Future

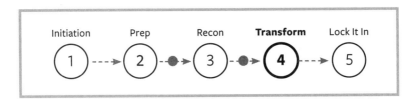

Initiation	Prep	Recon	**Transform**	Lock It In
①	②	③	④	⑤

IT IS TIME to bring the future to life. We have arrived at the Transformation Program, phase 4 of our journey. This is where activities identified in Recon will be broken down into further detail, mapped out in all their glorious complexity, and set into motion. This is where the new world is constructed.

When you have a transformation on your hands, it can be deadly to treat it like a normal project and operate as usual. On paper, a transformation looks like a big, complex set of interconnected projects.

It can be deadly to treat a transformation like a normal project and operate as usual.

That is daunting enough. But the reality can be even more intimidating. Much more than a set of projects, transformation is the architecting or rearchitecting of an entire system of people. It is the envisioning and creation of a new world. It is the act of leading people on a journey to a future state, while maintaining an unrelenting focus on business value.

Whether you are the executive sponsor or the transformation leader, there are some critical things you must know (and do) to ensure your Transformation Program moves quickly and does not unintentionally bleed business value. I will guide you through them and across a couple more pitfalls (yes, more pitfalls—you knew this was a perilous endeavor when you started!).

Due to your foresight and diligence in conducting a Recon Mission, you have the foundation to move fast. You have in your possession the skeleton of a transformation map from which to begin. Expectations have been set, and the foundation for organizational ownership has been laid. You are well prepared. It is time to begin the Transformation Program.

WAIT. SUPPOSE... I DIDN'T CONDUCT A RECON MISSION?

What's that, you say? You did not conduct a Recon Mission? But you are committed and have allocated the funding, so you jumped ahead?

What happened? Maybe you hit a tipping point, where after many months—or years—of circular conversation, the CEO finally became fed up with organizational inertia and abruptly pulled the trigger. Or perhaps the organization is reacting to an external event that makes it imperative to get going. Right now. Maybe a competitor's action. A new regulation. A global crisis. Perhaps your organization has new ownership. Or a new CEO or divisional head has been brought on board with the expectation of bringing great change and is taking decisive action.

Whatever the reason, you are committed and you have funding, but you have not conducted a Recon Mission. And right now, you want to run full speed ahead. You're being asked how quickly you can deliver. You hear the siren call of detailed Transformation Program work, urging you to dive right in. You think you are doing the right thing. But in all likelihood, you are not setting up your transformation to survive in the long run. Does this sound familiar? You are being lured into the deadly Too Deep, Too Soon pitfall (see page 97). Because you did not invest in solid Reconnaissance work, you are on shaky ground for execution. You are lacking a well-thought-out, mid-level view of the future state. You have no roadmap and no team members who understand what to do. You have not set expectations across the organization. And almost assuredly, you are lacking even a shadow of broader organizational ownership. These things will come back to haunt you.

But it doesn't have to be that way.

Freeze. Stop right there. We can recover from this.

As quickly as possible, rescue anyone who has fallen into the pit. Go back to the last section. Review the guidance for conducting your Reconnaissance Mission. If you missed any preparation steps, execute those as well. If you need to save face, refer to all of this Preparation and Reconnaissance work as the first phase of your Transformation Program. Funnel in what you know, assemble the team, and build out that mid-level understanding and roadmap. Set expectations. Widely communicate the game plan across the executive team. As you near the end of this work, begin assembling the larger crew for the full Transformation Program.

In this chapter, I discuss the most critical and least understood dynamics of executing a Transformation Program. The overarching priorities right now are to move fast, maintain commitment, and not lose sight of business value as the future state is built out.

First, you need to set up the team for speed and focus, which involves utilizing the talent you already gathered in Recon. Second, we will discuss the most common ways that programs bleed business value during this phase. Third, we'll talk about commitment. It will be crucial to reinforce commitment during this phase. Then grab your cape—your superpower, activated during Recon, also plays an important role in the Transformation Program. Following that, we will round out the chapter with some masterful maneuvers in program operations.

If you have taken Preparation and Reconnaissance seriously—and communicated a compelling Transformation Story—then you have a solid foundation from which to execute this Transformation Program. That does not mean it will be easy—this will be a lot of hard work and there remain perils yet to uncover. But you have put yourself in the best position possible for success. So grab your gear, we're off to build the future!

Setting Up the Team for Speed and Focus

A Transformation Program is a big, complex set of interconnected projects, interacting with an even more complex people system. This is already challenging. But it is further complicated by the fact that it is running in concert with many other events and activities beyond the control of the program team. There may be other company initiatives underway within the greater corporate umbrella. Ongoing operations has needs. External events occur: A regulation changes and suddenly you lose access to your legal expert for two weeks. A tsunami hits Japan, and one of your vendors can no longer get the parts necessary to complete their work. Your program is complex not only because it is coordinating its own many activities, but also because it is constantly adapting and responding to new information and events.

This complex undertaking requires a great Transformation team, one with strong Transformation Program management expertise. Make sure you have it. Take a moment to refresh your memory on the advanced transformation know-how required, as conveyed in the fourth law (see page 39). Keep that in mind as we dive into what you really need to know about a highly effective Transformation Program. It's transformation time.

OFF TO A FAST START WITH THE RECON TEAM

The Recon team will provide the core of your Transformation team. You secured top talent for Recon, and those individuals are excellent candidates for leadership roles in your Transformation Program. Not only are they some of the most talented professionals in the company, but they have developed a deep understanding of what lies in front of you. Critically, they also possess a strong sense of ownership. That Recon team includes not only experts in the business, but also experts in program management who are all fully apprised of the challenge at hand. They are orchestrators who live by the laws of transformation and have, for the past few months, been immersed in this challenge, this organization, this people system.

Furthermore, your Recon team members have already bonded and learned to work with one another. Transferring many of them onto the Transformation team will pave the way for the team to smoothly establish operating routines and collaborate effectively from day one. You may choose not to keep everyone from the Recon team. And not everyone you do keep will be a fit for the most senior program roles— some may be better suited for other roles. But you will certainly be able to form a powerful core starter team.

Regardless of how many Recon team members you deploy, you will certainly need to supplement with additional team members. As you add members to build out the full team, recognize that you have some great once-in-a-lifetime career opportunities here. You should easily be able to draw in more top talent. There are analysis and coordination roles for junior talent, workstream leadership roles for managerial talent, and senior subject matter expert roles for experienced professional talent.

CAN YOU USE CONSULTANTS FOR PROGRAM EXECUTION?

During the Transformation Program, there are many ways to effectively engage consultants and other third parties—as long as you do not outsource ownership (see page 107 to review that pitfall). By the very nature of the world we live in today, no one has in-house expertise for everything. Therefore, the vast majority of the work here is likely to be executed by consultants or vendors. Depending on the complexity and scale of your transformation, you may hire quite a few outside firms, from legal to technical, in order to get the specialization necessary for different elements of your transformation. You will be buying tools and technology, hiring experts and advisors.

Regardless of how insourced or outsourced your team is, one of the most valuable external engagements is the addition of an experienced transformation advisor or coach. Find a great transformation advisor and put them on retainer for the duration of the program. If they are really good, and you have built a solid Transformation team, you will only need about 20 percent of their time (eight to ten hours per week).

Transformation Programs also require a lot of coordination, and it is easy to acquire that type of support from consultants, if you choose. You may directly hire many companies, or just a couple and rely on them to subcontract the majority of the additional consultants and vendors. That's fine, but in order to effectively deliver your program, you must maintain ownership of it all.

Go ahead and hire the external firms you need to handle various segments of work, but the core Transformation team (and of course, the transformation leader) must understand that they own this. The people leading your transformation efforts must truly care about the future of your organization. In order to retain that critical organizational ownership and connection, your core program team—the transformation leadership team—should be composed primarily of employees.

No matter how you choose to construct the various components of your future—regardless of the proportion of work outsourced, off-shore, built or bought, distributed or collocated, executed by boutique consultancies or large systems integrators—do not attempt to out-source ownership. It will not end well.

ORGANIZATIONAL CHANGE MANAGEMENT BEGINS EARLY

It should not surprise you that I am a big proponent of organizational change management. Back in Initiation, we began by talking about people and systems of people, because they are at the core of any successful transformation. This holds true throughout the entirety of our journey. This Transformation Program is not just introducing new products, processes, and tools. It is shaping an entire system of people. Accordingly, it requires a significant amount of organizational change management. This will begin now and extend through the final phase of our journey.

What do I mean by organizational change management? Time spent thoughtfully considering the impact of the move to the future state—specifically, the impact it will have on people. Time spent strategizing over how best to bring those people along on the journey into the new world. Mapping out new jobs. Detailing the changes to existing jobs. Helping people understand and learn their new world. Form a group of dedicated people to do this.

Organizations are notorious for underinvesting in this. Establish a workstream dedicated to organizational change management. Put someone in charge who is savvy about people systems. To assure collective ownership and collaboration, assign shared ownership between that workstream leader and all the other workstream leaders.

In theory, ownership for organizational change management can be embedded within each individual workstream. In practice, this distributed approach rarely works well, resulting in insufficient attention to the system of people that you are transforming. In a complex transformation, it leads to disjointed, confusing communications. In a less complex transformation, the need to transform the people system is typically forgotten altogether, as tactical concerns are given priority. After all, it's just a small transformation, right? How hard can it be? We'll just implement some new technology and new business value will magically manifest—but wait, remember the Just Technology pitfall (see page 67)? The magic never happens without concerted effort put into the people system.

The goal of organizational change management is easy to define. It is to make sure that people—people at all levels—are taking the journey to achieve the intended business value. People must:

- Know that they need to change

- Know why they need to change

- Be able to envision the change

- Be able to imagine themselves operating in the changed world

- Strive to create real value out of the new world

We will get into some specific techniques later, in phase 5. For now, establish the workstream and let this team begin mapping roles and planning ways in which people will best absorb the new world.

ESTABLISH A CULTURE OF SHARED OWNERSHIP

As the Transformation team begins to plan achievement of the future, let's kick this off right by setting expectations about culture.

Make no mistake, you need this transformation to succeed. The future of the organization depends upon it. Therefore, regardless of your company culture, you must establish the right mindset for the Transformation Program team. This journey will be arduous and long, often taking years to complete, and the program culture must be able to hold strong throughout.

You must grant the team authority. And you must instill in them an empowering set of expectations that clearly convey how they will behave and how it should feel to be part of the program. There are specific core principles the team must live by to make it through

the challenging journey ahead. Following are the five components that I have proven form a highly effective Transformation team culture.

Driven by business value: Above all, this team must be founded on the principle that their reason for existence is the achievement of valuable business outcomes. Over the course of the journey, they will encounter many tough decisions and trade-offs, be driven toward dangerous pitfalls, and get distracted by devious dragons. Meanwhile, the world continues to move forward. With this principle forming the foundation, the team will maintain focus and urgency, and approach solutioning and decision-making to maximize business value. If the achievement of valuable business outcomes is not clearly established as their purpose, then it becomes tempting for any team, when under pressure, to repeatedly prioritize cost and time over business value.

> *The team must be founded on the principle that their reason for existence is the achievement of valuable business outcomes.*

Autonomy, authority, accountability: Autonomy, authority, and account-ability must be bestowed upon the team, then nurtured and enabled by the transformation leader and the executive sponsor. The team must take these things to heart and not be tentative or intimidated.

The best Transformation teams are open to the possible.

They need to know that while they do not have all the answers, they possess the power to find the answers. And that they have the power to hold people accountable—both inside and outside of the program team—for meeting commitments.

Shared ownership: Shared ownership is the heart of the team. Having this means never saying "it's not my job." It means keeping the overarching business goals in mind and naturally collaborating—constantly—to make things happen. Collaborating not with the intent to check boxes. Not to prove certain people were involved. Instead, collaborating for the express purpose of solving problems, building ownership, and driving progress.

Shared ownership pumps blood through the operation and keeps everyone engaged. A culture of genuine shared ownership has far-reaching power to influence well beyond the program team. When you have this, Transformation team members will naturally draw in others throughout the organization and engage them in the mission. This attitude, combined with transformation know-how, can create positive reinforcing loops that build organizational ownership.

Open to the possible: Complementing shared ownership, and no less important, is the specific growth-focused mindset of being open to the possible. This mindset enables the team to tackle any challenge. It also makes them uniquely sensitive to "the way we've always done it," and they will constantly overturn this orthodoxy to see what lies beneath. "Hey, if we remove this rationale, what's possible now?"

When we remove "the way we've always done it" as a valid reason, everything can be reimagined. Reinvented. Redesigned. Revolutionary customer experiences can be created. Decades-old processes become unnecessary. Roles can change, and organizations can adapt. With this mindset, the team is open to all possibilities. They will always question the need to continue doing something as is, and they will consistently be able to adapt and conquer new challenges. The best Transformation teams are open to the possible.

Determined to make it work: A deep-rooted determination to deliver runs through any successful Transformation team. Challenges are expected. These are a normal part of the job in the land of transformation. These challenges *will* be conquered. There is no doubt about it. The team is confident in their ability to persevere, no matter what death-defying feats must be performed. They will leverage the unique strengths, knowledge, and connections of every individual on their team. Furthermore, they will tap into the strengths of the entire organization. And they will fearlessly drive forward to rapidly recognize options and trade-offs, in order to make the future possible.

Combine all of these elements together, and then overlay the laws of transformation to form a resilient foundational culture. A culture equipped to lead great change. Build this culture and reinforce it constantly. This provides the energy that will power your transformation through turbulent seas, enable it to outsmart the dragons plotting to take down your ships, and allow it to glide over pitfalls with ease, like the one nearby.

Pitfall Advisory #7: Cutting Business Value

There will come a time when a trade-off must be made. Wait. Let's be brutally honest. There will come *many* times when trade-offs must be made. Times when budget estimates turn out to be way too low, when it's clear timelines will not be met, or when it is discovered that some future state element just cannot be brought to life the way it was envisioned.

In this situation, most programs face the challenge through the lens of the traditional triangle of time, budget, and scope. Will you increase the budget? Increase the timeline? Reduce the scope? Or some combination thereof? Cutting scope in order to keep cost and timing on target is tempting. *Very* tempting. After all, time and cost are much more visible measures. It feels like a quick fix to cut scope. But this is dangerous. And addictive. Scope is where the business value lives. Repeatedly prioritizing cost and time will slowly squeeze the business value out of the program—the business value that, sadly, was the very reason for the transformation in the first place. Transformations led by technology professionals are especially susceptible to this pitfall, as they do not always recognize the significance of the business value being discarded.

To combat this, it is critical that the program team's purpose be clearly established foremost as the achievement of valuable business outcomes. And that these types of decisions are not allowed to occur in isolation.

When such difficult decision points arise, it is vital that the discussion starts from the beginning of your transformation: with the vision. Why are you on this journey in the first place? What is this transformation intended to achieve? Then walk it forward: What future state elements are in jeopardy here? What are the options for achieving them, given where you are at? There should be some thoughtful options created—not simply "add time, add cost, cut scope." Only once real options are on the table is it the time for the decision makers to discuss the options and trade-offs—and decide how to resolve the situation. Once made, such decisions should be clearly documented. Executive sponsors, review these and watch for a pattern—you need to know if the business value is slowly and quietly bleeding out of your transformation.

Maximizing the Value of Your Cyborg

You've confidently catapulted over the Cutting Business Value pitfall and are feeling pretty smug. But that is not the only thing threatening to drain your business value. There is another popular and pervasive way in which business value is lost, hiding at the intersection of people and technology. This one is not exactly a pitfall. It's more of an omnipresent reality. And it requires vigilance.

There is an exciting future to achieve, and chances are, delivering on the promise of that future state includes some technology. Perhaps a lot of technology. And if that technology is not executed effectively in conjunction with the people system, a Transformation Program can unintentionally lose much of its anticipated business value.

Your business transformation will introduce and reshape a multitude of technological and human elements as it changes existing structures and produces new ones. Hidden within the intersection of technology and humanity lies great potential for business value to be realized or lost. To realize the greatest business value, people and technology must flow together and reinforce one another, seamlessly handing work back and forth between the steps of your business processes.

Think about the intersections where humans pass off a process to a machine or vice versa. Let's start with an everyday example: interacting with a smartphone. Ever find yourself painfully watching as a friend or relative awkwardly fumbles through their new (or not-so-new) phone's features? Now imagine that in your business.

First, consider something tangible. Think about places where humans literally receive a physical part produced by a machine and handle final packaging and transport. The fluidity of that process directly affects how quickly a product can be delivered to a customer and revenue collected. That may seem obvious. Now for something more esoteric.

How about someone interpreting data? Consider a sales analyst at work. What data their sales systems collect and how it is presented can have a big impact. At the same time, how a sales analyst thinks about the world can also have a great impact. Brought together, the combination of data and analysis generates value. Or misses an opportunity. Potentially a great opportunity. How sales data is analyzed and interpreted has great implications for pricing, positioning, and decisions to build additional products. Is the data presented in a useful way? Does the analyst use the right data? How do they interpret it? Do the human and machine interact effectively?

Similarly, how people decide to train a machine learning model, and choose what information to feed it, has significant implications for the effectiveness and quality of the model's outputs. In turn, the way those outputs are interpreted and used can have a wide range of impacts. There have been many famous examples of machine learning models reinforcing racial and gender bias. This demonstrates that at the intersection of humans and technology, it is possible to not only create value or miss opportunities but also unintentionally do harm. So be careful here.

Take a step back to see the fusion of people and technology. Further back. Keep going until you can see your entire organization—all of its many human and technological components—at once. From out here, it looks like one big machine. See the fusion of robotic components with the people system? Technology forms connections between people, from customers to suppliers, and between every function inside the organization. It passes information, completes tasks, moves parts, assembles products, and records a significant portion of everything we do. It also enhances our ability to operate, giving us superhuman powers to produce more and more all the time for a given amount of time and energy. I have said that organizations are people systems, which is true, but we need to expand that paradigm slightly to acknowledge that these days, that people system is starting to look a lot like a cyborg.

This has critical implications for your Transformation Program. A cyborg loses its powers if robotic and human components are not smoothly integrated. Likewise, significant business value can be lost if the technological and human components of your increasingly automated organization are not smoothly integrated.

Unfortunately, in many companies, technology is treated—and behaves—as a silo unto itself. In a heavily digital world, this can create significant tension and inefficiency in driving increased business value. This tension quickly becomes amplified during a transformation. Your transformation may not be setting out to solve that for the long term (maybe your next one should?), but it is critical to acknowledge this legacy mindset and forge a different path for the execution of the program.

How will you enable your future state cyborg to realize the true value of its powers? How will you avoid disconnected joints and poorly functioning limbs? If your natural inclination is to create isolated technology workstreams, you are not alone. But don't do that. Now, more than ever, running technology development off in its own silo means leaving business value on the table. Regardless of how an organization has been operating day-to-day, the Transformation Program needs to run as one business-focused team.

Part of the solution is to design workstreams with clear business goals, which may mean having technology components embedded in a number of places. That's OK. You are gaining the benefit of focused business value delivery. The greatest reason for centralized technology functions is to achieve economies of scale from ongoing technology operations—that benefit does not apply in the operation of a Transformation Program.

Structuring the teams well is important, but even more critical is having the right mindset in those teams. Ultimately, the key lies in the culture of transformation (see page 148). The achievement of business value *must* be clearly established as the goal of this program across all workstreams.

And there must be strong business ownership, regardless of how many moving parts—functions, locations, people, suppliers, activities—there are in your particular transformation. Your transformation is almost certainly hiring one or more (perhaps many more) technology vendors. This creates an even greater likelihood of executing isolated technology work. It is time to revisit our outsourcing discussion from earlier. Let's recap: You cannot outsource ownership. Remember

Love it or hate it, technology is part of you.

that? You own this transformation, and you are ultimately accountable. Those consultants work for you. Engage with that in mind. As contracts are negotiated and vendors onboarded, there is the opportunity to influence how your teams will interact with their teams. Set expectations. Organizations spend a lot of time negotiating time, cost, and deliverable quality metrics, and not nearly enough on the factors that make or break business value creation. Take the opportunity to lay out a business-focused, collaborative approach from the start, and create partnerships where engaged business owners work closely with the consultants.

Love it or hate it, technology is part of you. It is a part of the people system. Every organization is a cyborg: a meld of human and technological components. Technology cannot be divorced from functions like operations or customer engagement, though organizations will often attempt to handle it that way. Significant business value will be gained or lost at the points where your people system interacts with digital systems and mechanical systems. A transformation must take that into account or risk leaking business value as the future state is constructed.

SO, I'LL BUILD IT AND I'LL SEE YOU ONCE IT'S DONE ?

NOT THIS TIME. LET'S TRY SOMETHING DIFFERENT.

@TUGLUS

Reinforcing Commitment

Transformations fail because people either do not know how to transform or are not truly committed. Or both. We discussed this in the Introduction (see page 7), and now—during the Transformation Program—is an important time to check in on commitment and think about how to keep it.

By this point in our journey, a great leader has been hired, as described in chapter 2 (see page 76). That leader has brought together a high-caliber team with business knowledge and expert Transformation Program management capability. They have the right know-how, and they have begun a Transformation Program. But we must not forget that knowing how to transform is meaningless without the actual commitment to support it. Both know-how and commitment are essential to maintain throughout the journey, and if either drops too low, for too long, the dragons—and your competitors—will win. That long-sought-after business value will never materialize, making you just another failed transformation statistic.

At this time, a transformation has two initial sources of commitment. First, the formal commitment to execute the program that was secured recently, through the Transformation Story. Which is great. But just because the executive team signed off on this, it does not mean that everyone is truly on board. In fact, some probably are not. Furthermore, commitment can fade, and often does.

The second source of commitment is the seeds of organizational ownership that were planted back in Recon. When you brought in highly talented individuals from various business groups, you inherited a connection to the executives who own those business areas. In most cases, they will want those people to succeed, regardless of how they feel about the Transformation Program.

You can choose to nurture or neglect that initial commitment. And make no mistake, if you choose to do nothing, then by default you have chosen neglect.

So, you are not starting from zero. You have some commitment. But commitment is neither guaranteed nor eternal. It will drop as new attractions arise, and fade over time with organizational fatigue, as discussed in the fourth law of transformation (see page 39). Once granted initial commitment to begin the Transformation Program, you have a choice. You can choose to nurture or neglect that initial commitment. And make no mistake, if you choose to do nothing, then by default you have chosen neglect. Commitment must be intentionally cultivated into a strong force and maintained throughout the remainder of the transformation journey.

What level of commitment do you really have right now? Let's find out. As the Transformation team is recruited, valuable information is being provided to you regarding where the broader organization actually stands in its commitment to this transformation. As you pull in talent from around the organization—leaders, business analysts, business data experts, technology experts, trainers, and so on—ask yourself a few questions: What level of talent is being offered to this program? How much of a fight is required in order to secure the right people for the program? How often are the right people deemed "too important" or "too critical" to be pulled away from what they are doing?

Battles for staffing reveal the current state of commitment. The answers to these questions will demonstrate where commitment sits right now: who is committed and how strong that commitment is. If weak talent is offered, and it requires significant effort to negotiate for strong talent, then this is a reflection of low commitment. The transformation is not being taken seriously and given priority.

You must assess the state of commitment and take action. Where the seeds have not taken root, replanting will be necessary. Weak areas, untended, will almost certainly pose challenges and resistance throughout the program, as the Transformation team seeks information, resources, and other support.

Even if you ascertain that you have a high level of commitment, this will not sustain on its own. It must be tended and actively managed. The transformation leader and their team must regularly meet with key executives and influencers across the organization, sharing versions of the Transformation Story, reinforcing the criticality of the mission, thanking them for their support thus far, and reminding them of what is in it for them. These communication points, conducted effectively and consistently, are the means by which commitment is maintained at top leadership levels. Where good talent and support are being provided, be sure to positively reinforce that as well, and not take it for granted.

A Transformation team can also influence broader organizational commitment through their advanced know-how. The team is doing two types of work. First, the obvious work that you can easily see: designs, definitions, software, processes, machines, organizational charts, models, metrics, and more. Let's call this the delivery of the activities. The second is the work you cannot see as easily: setting and reinforcing expectations, negotiating, influencing, reconciling differences, and building ownership. This is the shaping of the people system.

Commitment can be reinforced through this second set of work. Of course, commitment must first exist to some degree, but great transformation leaders will take that fledgling commitment and work hard to extend and amplify it. Through communications such as targeted roadshows, videos, and newsletters, in combination with regular meetings with key groups and individuals, they will slowly build familiarity and reduce unknowns across the organization. They will apply their transformation know-how, leveraging their knowledge of people systems, relativity, and fear. They will share the urgency of an ever-moving world. The messages they spread are about shared ownership: "we're all in this together." Through this, they constantly find ways to move people toward a common vision of transformation and include them in their epic tales. In short, they lean heavily on their deep understanding of the laws of transformation to reinforce and grow commitment.

Nurture or neglect? It's your choice. It is unquestionably a lot of hard work and requires no small amount of persistence and determination. But if you allow commitment to drop precipitously low and linger there too long, your transformation will almost assuredly meet with an early demise. So, is it really a choice?

Superpower in Action

When we activated your superpower back in Recon, we used it in your Transformation Story to provide something familiar, to help secure commitment to a Transformation Program. Now that we are executing that program, we will continue to leverage your superpower. Not just to dispel fear, but to bring people together and engage them in the creation of their future.

Here is a little-known secret to successful transformation: Great transformation leaders are respectful of the past, even while building the future. Furthermore, they are not just respectful of it—they strategically and actively leverage it to move people toward the future. They know that this transformation will support and advance the superpower of the organization. They just have to connect the dots so others see it as clearly as they do. Nostalgic stories of the past, shared by employees with great pride, often speak to the superpower of an organization. Recognize this and you will discover many opportunities to connect your scary future state work to something familiar. When you are able to see the superpower contained within those stories, you can point out how that core shared purpose is, in fact, enduring. And that it will continue to flourish through—and in fact, even be advanced by—the transformation underway.

During the Transformation Program, we want to expand our understanding of that organizational superpower to identify nuances, extensions, and the particular language that resonates with different groups of people. Although I was able to sum up the superpower

Great transformation leaders are respectful of the past, even while building the future.

in my experience at the CDC neatly—that system of people all cared deeply about improving health care—it does not typically manifest that cleanly in practice. That does not mean it is any less powerful. You do not need everyone in the organization to use exactly the same words for them to have the same meaning. This is especially important in global organizations. A superpower is not a catchphrase. It is a shared purpose.

My experience with Henry Ford Learning Institute (HFLI) provides a great example of this. When I was advising HFLI, it was clear to me that they had an extremely strong superpower, yet no one described it precisely the same way.

HFLI is a nonprofit organization focused on innovation in education. All of their service offerings were designed around immersive, in-person learning that required the active engagement of participants. They had built an excellent global reputation around this. Then the COVID-19 pandemic hit, almost overnight eliminating the ability to conduct those in-person workshops and classes. This was a scary time for this organization, fraught with great unknowns. Not only was their future unknown, but so was the trajectory and ultimate impact of the pandemic on the entire world.

For a lesser organization, this could easily have marked their demise. But not HFLI. With great determination, they took stock of the current state and the disruption. They envisioned a new future and assessed techniques, tools, and processes that could get them there. And then they set out to achieve that, iteratively deploying and adjusting.

They were forced to rapidly and dramatically transform the entirety of their core service offering. Yet, remarkably, they preserved the core of what made those services unique. And it was all due to their superpower. HFLI's superpower is the deep-rooted belief that people experience deeper learning by doing. That to best educate and develop people—from children to adults of any age—true learning is accomplished by doing something, by actively engaging, experiencing, immersing.

When people at HFLI revealed their superpower to me, the words came out in a variety of ways: learning by doing, collaborative, community, immersive, active, engaging. Sometimes the words were expanded: immersive learning experiences ... to develop community leaders. Using all of these words, their transformation leader continually connected their superpower to their transformation goals as she led them in the creation of the future state. For a Transformation Program leader, it is important that you recognize the core purpose, here the belief in "deeper learning by doing." But do not change the superpower language of the people system, unless you really need to. It is more powerful in their own words. You are not there to develop brand marketing; you are there to build and shepherd people into the future state.

HFLI leveraged that superpower to propel them through their business transformation. They developed new educational approaches, designed new collaborative learning activities, introduced new roles, and employed technology in new ways. They created a brand new service offering: immersive and active educational experiences that are effectively led, and participated in, in an entirely virtual way. Where no one ever meets in person.

Never underestimate the strength of your superpower. This shared purpose gives people the energy and ability to come together to focus on the good of the whole as they deliver a new world. Take every opportunity to leverage it throughout your Transformation Program. Expect the precise wording to vary, as people are diverse. Expand your understanding of that organizational superpower to identify nuances, extensions, and the particular language that resonates with different groups of people.

What are threads of your corporate belief system that will endure and hold true into the future? What gives the people purpose? There is something about your company that makes it special. Fashion it into a lifeline that draws from the past, thrives in the present, and connects to the future. Leverage it. Amplify it. Embed it throughout the transformation and keep it at the forefront of people's thoughts. Bust out those capes and put that superpower into action!

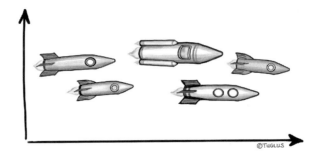

Operational Maneuvers: A Fleet of Rocket Ships

You need speed. You're deep into this now, and you're battling organizational fatigue and vigilantly monitoring the relentless progression of the world, all while working hard to deliver business value. Your Transformation Program must proceed rapidly to erect the future state, so let's build a fleet of rocket ships to get you there.

Imagine a typical Gantt chart of program management—you know the one, with the horizontal bars representing activities. In your mind, replace the bars with rocket ships. Perfect. Now all of your activities are rocket ships instead of boring bars. Isn't that better? OK, we're not doing this because I love science. And we're not going to take apart a rocket. Not today. We're doing this to help you envision what should be happening in the middle of a Transformation Program.

Running a program is like running a transportation company. A fleet of ships is built, in various sizes, to deliver all the components of the new world, also known as the future transformed state of your organization. A Transformation Program consists of hundreds, perhaps thousands, of ships. Myriad activities and outputs, all of which need to be connected, coordinated, and completed. To add further complexity, there will be some peak travel days (like holidays) where many activities converge to deliver something especially memorable: a tangible product, a regional platform deployment, or the first evolution of a new division.

Operating the Transformation Program is about effectively launching, flying, and landing those ships. In order to do that, you must successfully navigate regulations, coordinate resources, reroute around obstacles, avoid pitfalls, and outsmart dragons. As the program shifts into full delivery mode, program team leaders essentially become air traffic controllers.

You may be thinking, "Wait, why are we talking about this? I hired a great transformation leader and team. Why do I need to know anything about operating details?"

You are correct. If you are the executive sponsor, you do not need to understand the internal mechanics of rocket ships and rocket launch logistics. But I bet you would like to know what is happening when your ship is stuck on the tarmac. Or being rerouted mid-air. And I suspect you want to be prepared when facing disgruntled passengers and their complaints. Therefore, to effectively and confidently support your transformation, there are just a few key operational aspects I want you familiar with. No rocket science. Honest.

Here are three quick insights into the operational maneuvers of an effective Transformation Program, plus one quick stop for a pitfall selfie. (With you *outside* the pit. Or leaping over it. I hope.)

A CUSTOM FLEET: THE RIGHT ROCKET FOR EACH FLIGHT

A transformation is a diverse journey. Introducing new concepts and paradigms. Reengineering people systems. Rewiring processes, building new tools. Activities produce a wide diversity of outputs: designs, organizational structures, brand components, operational software, customer websites, new machinery, and more. Not every activity will, nor should it, follow the same process to delivery. Building a new online user experience? Perhaps you will bust out a classic agile software development methodology, like scrum or extreme programming. Need regulatory approval for a new product? I expect a fairly linear set of steps to satisfy the regulators. Maybe it seems obvious to you that these would be different. Yet many Transformation Programs try to force fit the same process to every activity. So come closer and we will study the perplexing One Process Fits All pitfall.

Pitfall Advisory #8: One Process Fits All

Take one part leadership enthusiasm for the latest trendy execution process, one part inexperienced transformation know-how, mix them together, and what do you get? Attempts to force fit a single approach to a diverse set of situations. Execution methodologies all have strengths and weaknesses. Never apply them indiscriminately to all situations, unless you want to waste a lot of time. (And if you want to waste a lot of time, there are far more pleasant ways to do that.) The One Process Fits All pitfall is a huge distraction and time sink. Do not forget—the world is moving! Taking the time to perfectly align everything, to introduce people to processes they are unfamiliar with, and to apply strict templates—it just doesn't make sense. This is a business transformation, not a science experiment. The goal here is business value, achieved as quickly and securely as possible. The goal is not program delivery process consistency.

This is another example of why it is crucial to hire experienced transformation leadership. They will know when to apply different delivery techniques and what type of ship to build (or buy) to deliver each activity. Executive sponsors, you must be aware of this pitfall, careful not to inadvertently put too much weight on the latest trend, and be ready to question a process bias if you see one. If you are the transformation leader, check your own process biases and those of your team. There are many distractions and dangers that are difficult to control over the course of a transformation, but this is not one of them. This one is fully within your control.

GROUND CONTROL MAY CHANGE YOUR DEPARTURE TIME

Expect a level of flux in the program schedule. Sometimes a ship is stuck on the tarmac. Maybe it is waiting for its pilots, who are on a delayed inbound flight. Or there is heavy snow. Mechanical failure. Rogue turtles on the runway. (This is a real problem at JFK—seriously.) Whatever the reason, ground control is actively working to get that ship launched, and more important, to make the most progress possible for the entire fleet. This means that when an activity's start date appears in jeopardy, the team should already, matter-of-factly, be evaluating plans B, C, and D: "Is there a way to keep the launch window? What other activities could be readied to begin instead? What are the dependencies? Can another rocket's launch time be moved up? What are the implications and downstream impacts if we do that?"

The Transformation team will collaborate with experts and impacted teams across the company to assess possible alternative plans, and handle all the downstream impacts as flight plans change. And that is exactly what you want to see happening: the team focused on maximizing overall delivery across the entire fleet, continually adjusting parallel activities to make progress wherever they can. Consequently, experts across the company will be called upon intermittently to solve problems, and their scheduled participation in various activities will change, as the activity plan will always experience a level of flux. Expect this.

AIR CONTROL MAY REROUTE YOUR FLIGHT

Unsurprisingly, challenges also arise while activities are in flight. A few years ago, I was on a plane from LA to Seattle. It had been a typical, uneventful flight, and we were preparing to land. A flight attendant came on over the intercom: "We have started our descent. In preparation for landing, please make sure your seat backs and tray tables are in their full upright position—we'll be on the ground in Spokane in twenty minutes."

I had been comfortably anticipating my arrival in Seattle, but in the silence that followed, I quickly shifted to startled comprehension as I realized the information provided was not quite what was expected: *OK, that sounds good... wait. What?!*

Passengers throughout the plane turned to look at each other. The attendant's announcement was the first indication that we would not, in fact, be landing in Seattle as expected, but would instead be landing in Spokane, 280 miles east of Seattle. After a few moments of intercom silence, the cabin filled with confused murmurs.

"Uh, did you hear . . .?"

"Did they say *Spokane*?"

"Wait, is this *not* the Seattle flight?"

A few minutes later, the intercom came to life again. An explanation was provided: Seattle was shrouded in thick fog, and all planes were being held. We would stop over in Spokane until Seattle ground control cleared us for takeoff.

This will happen during your Transformation Program.

Well, not literally ending up in Spokane. I hope. (Not that there is anything wrong with Spokane. If that is where you are trying to go.) Nor—hopefully—will you experience the awkwardly delayed explanation of the situation that was conveyed to surprised passengers. (That was a solid example of poor expectations management.) But the unanticipated challenges mid-air? Absolutely. You will definitely experience that during your transformation. That *will* happen to you.

When a challenge hits, air traffic control (your Transformation team leaders) will mobilize to solve the problem, pulling in experts from wherever needed. First, what are the options to keep the ship in the air? Maybe it is nothing more than a bad weather front, and the flight plan can be adjusted to divert the ship around it. Then it can remain in the air and continue on to the expected destination, simply arriving a little later than originally planned. But maybe that's not possible. So, more options are considered. And once all options to keep it in the air are exhausted, they look at grounding options. The best solution might be to put that activity on hold. In which case, the team will figure out how to execute that hold safely, in a way that enables the activity to be easily restarted at a later time (like landing in Spokane). And they will manage expectations along the way (unlike landing in Spokane).

Your team will know when to land in Spokane. They will know how to manage that. And how to communicate it. It is a success when such challenges are handled well, in ways that keep the overall program as healthy as possible.

There will be challenges. Subject matter expects will be called in, on the fly, to help solve them and plot a new course. Activities will be shifted around, causing resources to be called to duty at different times than originally planned. A good Transformation team will anticipate challenges, engage the right people, make necessary changes, and communicate effectively.

So, about those disgruntled passengers . . .

When other executives are making a fuss about schedule changes, the most likely culprit is poor communication—like the unfortunately surprising communication of a detour to Spokane, conveyed while we were already descending into Spokane. If the situation simply requires better communication, the transformation leader must fix that. However, these complaints may also signal a lack of support or ownership. Consider that and take appropriate action. If the complaints are purely political posturing, the transformation leader or the executive sponsor must kill it quickly. There is likely more complaining occurring than is visible. Understanding what should happen during your Transformation Program will equip you to handle critics and gauge when to be truly concerned.

And that's all you need to know about rocket ships.

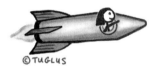

©TUGLUS

The journey is not over yet. As you enter the last few months—typically the last four to six months—of your Transformation Program, though you may not realize it, you are entering phase 5, the final phase of your transformation journey.

Before we talk about that, let me just say that if you have made it this far, congratulations on surviving to this point! The critical business value that you set out to create—is that still materially intact? If

The end of the Transformation Program is not the end of your transformation journey. The goal of a transformation is not to finish the program; the goal is to deliver the business value.

so, you are doing better than the vast majority of companies out there. Be sure to celebrate key milestones throughout the program, and, of course, the upcoming milestone marking the end of the Transformation Program. But when you hit that particular milestone, know that your journey is not over yet. As the future is brought to life, it is easy to believe that the conclusion of the program is the end of the journey. It is not. If you mistakenly believe that, a lot of unrealized business value is about to be left on the table.

During the final few months of the Transformation Program, as the last of the program activities are nearing their conclusion, there is a lot going on. This can be a stressful period. It is filled with tying things together, putting out last minute fires, assembling those last pieces of the future state, and getting them put in place and connected. Often the program will culminate in a final big launch of a new product, platform, or division. At this point, many leaders become laser-focused on all of those details, to the exclusion of all else, expending all their time and energy on completing the final activities in the Transformation Program roadmap. Although perfectly understandable, this myopic focus is actually quite dangerous. The end of the Transformation Program is not the end of your transformation journey. The goal of a transformation is not to finish the program; the goal is to deliver the business value. And we haven't done that yet. Perhaps partially, but not completely. Further actions must be taken that are absolutely essential to realize the potential of your transformation.

Therefore, as you are completing the last of the program activities, the final phase of the journey must be put in motion simultaneously. Actions must be taken to start locking in the value of this transformation, starting right now, months before the program ends. Let's head over to phase 5 to see what that looks like.

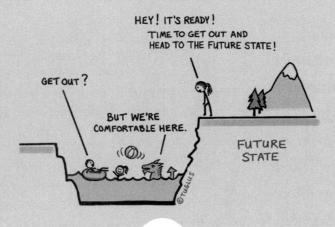

5
Lock It In
Secrets to Securing Business Value

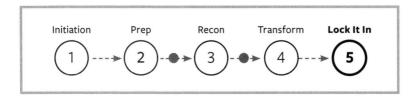

Initiation — Prep — Recon — Transform — **Lock It In**

(1) - - -> (2) -●-> (3) -●-> (4) - - -> (5)

THE TRANSFORMATION PROGRAM may be ending, but our journey is not over. Be honest. Did you think we were done? Are you exhausted just thinking about more? At this point, the work remaining to lock in the value of your transformation is not complicated. The activities require some thought and people-savvy but are not overly complex. However, they *do* require perseverance and determination at a time when energy is low.

It is absolutely possible to conquer all of the challenges up to this point and still fail to deliver real business value. You must lock it in.

By now you have made significant progress in turning your initial vision into an attainable future state. Hard-fought, long-awaited changes are beginning to come to life across the organization. New processes instituted. New technology implemented. Organizational structures blown up and redesigned. New roles and responsibilities rolled out. New cultural expectations introduced.

Your future state is beginning to look real. But if you are serious about achieving business value, it is not yet time to claim success. Your transformation goals are by no means secured. It is absolutely possible to conquer all of the challenges up to this point and still fail to deliver real business value. You must lock it in. This final phase of our journey, Lock It In, is vital to securing your business value. Organizational fatigue—and Transformation team fatigue—is threatening. There are deadly pitfalls and distracting dragons nearby. But you have come this far. Now lock it in.

Being the executive leading a transformation is very different from being the executive who inherits the transformed world. I've seen both sides. In fact, I've even seen both sides of the same transformation—taking leadership over the future state of a transformation I had successfully led. So I know what is needed to really make a transformation stick.

This particular transformation was a highly successful multiyear, $100M+ global journey where I transformed the entire core operations of a company. Subsequently, I became the executive in charge of global product delivery, and then not long after, over all of the business operations that had been transformed. This uniquely positioned me to identify first-hand the most effective actions for locking in the business value of a transformation. I knew what actions had been taken during the transformation, I knew precisely what potential this new world held, and now I was in the position to take full advantage and act upon it.

The business value delivered by the transformation was powerful, providing capabilities that could dramatically improve time to market, flexibility, operational speed, customer experience, and quality. As the head of business operations, I was able to leverage this newly transformed organization to deliver products to market five to ten times faster. And to offer services to our clients that no competitor was able to bring to market for years thereafter. This was exactly the business value we had envisioned achieving.

By sitting in that position, leading the future state, while also knowing what was possible because I had led the transformation, it was clear to me how to take advantage of those new capabilities and bring that business value to life. But in retrospect, it is also clear just how many ways I could have missed or avoided taking advantage of that potential. How easy it would have been to continue operating with the same mindset as before, and produce little additional value, even while faithfully using the new tools and processes.

Let's talk about what it takes to lock in the value of a transformation. It should not surprise you that it all revolves around people. Employees must develop confidence and expertise in the new world, and ownership must migrate from the Transformation Program leadership to the ongoing operational business leadership. Throughout, the second law of transformation (see page 26) is more relevant than ever as we battle a familiar foe: the fear of the unknown.

It would be unwise to underinvest in this final phase, having come this far. This will become obvious shortly, as we cross two unbelievably treacherous pitfalls. In this phase, I will guide you through how to immerse employees in the new world, engage your secret weapon (yes, you have one), deploy your superpower for maximum impact (you did bring your cape, right?), and, finally, execute a heart transplant to lock in ownership. We will, of course, be checking vital signs throughout to ensure the patient—your organization—comes through this with flying colors. What's that, you say? Sounds like a visit to the secret laboratory of an evil mastermind? Hmm. No, no, of course not. But I will need you to put on this blindfold and place all your electronics in this steel mesh bag... and let's remove the word "evil," shall we?

DON'T LET IT OVERWHELM YOU

Before we head over to the survival studies laboratory, let's pause for a moment. I realize that this can all be a bit overwhelming. If you are early in your journey of transformation, do not get too far ahead of yourself. Practically speaking, there is no need to obsess over these survival strategies too far in advance. Although they are essential, there are also extremely dangerous pitfalls earlier in your journey that can destroy much—or all—of your transformation's value before you even reach this point. So first, put your energy into executing a strong Preparation phase and Recon Mission. Then get your Transformation Program up and running effectively. Once your rocket operations are in motion, use your organizational change management workstream to put some intense effort into planning out this phase of the journey.

Ready to master this final phase and complete your transformation? Let's lock it in. As we enter, there is a powerful pitfall nearby, lying in wait. One you would be wise to be wary of. Let's cautiously approach and study the Unrealized Potential pitfall.

Pitfall Advisory #9: Unrealized Potential

Although a wonderful new world has been architected, there are no guarantees that the organization, the people system (yes, that again), will truly leverage this new world to drive the business forward. The Transformation Program has provided employees with new constructs, flexibility, automation, and access, but how will you get them to take full advantage of it? How will you be sure to avoid ending up in situations like the following?

Imagine that a new division has been set up and is expected to provide great synergy with existing businesses—to cross-sell products and services, and to jointly create new ones. However, a year goes by and no collaborations emerge between the new division and other divisions.

At another company, a new operating platform is launched, including new software and robotics, that provides impressive capabilities for automation with the power to decrease manufacturing time and increase product quality. Some features are never turned on, and employees try their best to conduct processes the same way they did before, printing schematics and including steps that no longer need to be completed manually.

Meanwhile, across the continent, a new product is launched at another company. Based on market and consumer research, this product has the potential to outsell every other existing product in that company. Unfortunately, it is given low priority for marketing and external communications, and provided limited sales support, stunting its ability to grow.

And at yet another organization, an innovation portfolio of investments in cutting-edge technologies has been formed. It is intended as a vehicle to incorporate new disruptive technologies into the business lines and create new offerings. Yet a year later, beyond the occasional prototype, none of the business units are meaningfully testing the technologies or applying any of them to create new value for their divisions.

These organizations have all landed squarely in the Unrealized Potential pitfall. What is especially devious about this pitfall is that, at first, it may not feel like a pitfall at all. There is a lot that is new and shiny right now in the future state—new processes, new tools, a little laminated card with new cultural pillars. Maybe even some nice new office equipment. It feels as though things are different. And yet the people have not changed. So they do not take advantage of all the potential of this new shiny land. Consequently, the business value of the transformation does not materialize.

In all examples, the future state has been delivered as ordered. The vision is clear. Yet the actual value of the transformation has not been fully realized. It is tragic when an organization gets all the way to this point in their journey, dodging dragons and leaping over pitfalls, solidly delivering all the tangible elements of the future state, only to fail to attain the expected value. Assuming the world did not change dramatically while the journey was taking place, it is almost certain that important steps were not taken to lock in the value. Unfortunately, many companies assume that the value will materialize on its own. They severely underinvest in this phase of the journey. This is unwise. You will know better.

A transformation is not truly complete until the underlying people system has been fully transformed. Completing the transformation of the people system requires an intense effort to reduce fear and build mastery in the new world, which runs throughout the Lock In period. There are great unknowns being revealed, and true commitment to the new world cannot be gained without dispelling fear. Knowledge, expertise, and confidence in the new world must be built to remove fear and realize the business potential. And ownership must be transferred.

Cementing and sustaining a newly transformed state requires far more effort than anyone likes to acknowledge. But as I mentioned earlier, it is not complicated. Let's set up our not-so-secret, not-at-all-evil laboratory, and move forward with locking this transformation in.

A transformation is not truly complete until the underlying people system has been fully transformed.

Immersing Employees in the New World

The faster an organization masters its new world, the faster the business value of the transformation will be realized. Unfortunately, most training activities—assuming training is even provided—fail to truly engage employees in a way that leads to mastery.

It is a common mistake to deploy training as a one-time, check-the-box activity. Employees are sent to a class for a few hours, or maybe a day or two. There they are asked to memorize new processes and quickly absorb how new systems and tools work. They are led through some exercises. Perhaps they are provided with a card detailing the new process or the new cultural norms. At the end of the class, they receive a certificate of completion. Done. They're ready.

But are they really? Probably not. And they are the lucky ones. Many new roles receive no training at all. Most training activities are technically accurate, logically executed, and efficiently rolled out to a narrowly identified audience. In the normal course of business, this type of training may be adequate. Because in that relatively static environment, a new employee will be surrounded by people who have already mastered the current state world. There will be many people to learn from and many people around to keep everything running well as the new employees are learning. In contrast, in a transformation, everyone is learning a new world all at once. There is no built-in support structure in the future state. It's all new to everyone. Consequently, a more intense and comprehensive approach to training is required.

For maximum absorption, people must be immersed in the new world, repeatedly, with increasing depth over time. The best immersive experiences incorporate the laws of transformation, bringing focus to the people and away from a myopic fixation on checklists and sign-offs. Effective immersion relies on a true understanding of people, and if we are being honest about people, we know that learning takes time. Time to dispel fear and execute the repetition necessary. Learning something totally new is not easy. This is why the Lock In activities, including immersion, must begin months prior to the conclusion of the Transformation Program and not end until months beyond the program launch date.

The faster an organization masters its new world, the faster the business value of the transformation will be realized.

Let's take a moment to explore this, because it is important to take to heart. How long does it take you to change a habit in your personal life? To adopt an exercise regime, change a diet, quit smoking? According to a study[3] from the University College London, it takes anywhere from 18 to 254 days, and on average 66 days. You and I both know that systems of people are even more complex than individuals, and what we are doing here is changing the habits of an entire people system.

The best immersion is people-centric, fear reducing, and relativity savvy, while reminding everyone that urgency is required and showcasing how epic this journey is. Here are some tips for leveraging the laws of transformation in your immersion:

People-centered (Law #1: It's all people systems): Slowly immerse people by providing content in easily consumable quantities. Often training is crammed into a short time period and includes too much

---

[3] "How Are Habits Formed," *European Journal of Social Psychology* 40, no. 6 (2010): 998–1009. http://repositorio.ispa.pt/bitstream/10400.12/3364/1/IJSP_998-1009.pdf.

new content for a brain to absorb at once. Design a set of experiences that each time extend deeper and further, instead of a single training event. Introduce and reinforce knowledge and capability over time. Include flexibility for different learning speeds and styles—online and on-demand sessions will allow people to learn at their own speed. For roles that are less regimented, conduct a series of guided conversations where employees engage in the ultimate definition of the roles.

Fear reducing (Law #2: People fear the unknown): Dispelling fear is an essential part of effective immersion. The scariest new things (in other words, the greatest unknowns), as viewed from the perspective of the employees, must be identified and given the proper priority and focus.

Relativity savvy (Law #3: Relativity reduces fear): Relativity is a powerful tool that can dispel fear by making new concepts more relatable. When people are taught how they are expected to operate within the new world, compare this to something familiar whenever possible. What parts are similar to prior roles? What is not changing? Do other people somewhere in the organization have similar roles? Can you bring in speakers who have been through a similar journey, operate in a similar environment, or use similar tools?

Urgent and epic (Law #4: You need speed and Law #5: You are writing an epic tale): Why is everyone on this journey? Employees must know that they are fighting against an ever-changing world and that they are part of an epic journey to transform this organization in powerful ways. That they are, in fact, an integral part of the success this organization is about to achieve. Do they know that? Make sure that they do.

Transformation success is all about understanding your system of people. People need help to change habits or form new ones. And cementing those changes takes repetition and time. Allow people to live and breathe the new world. To immerse themselves in it. Take advantage of advanced technology to develop augmented and virtual reality experiences. With a little ingenuity, you can combine low-tech and high-tech techniques to create compelling, immersive learning experiences. Challenge your learning and development professionals.

Throughout immersion, employees should feel themselves get closer and closer to the new world, in a way that makes them more and more comfortable and adept at operating in the future state. Make the future state as real as possible before the Transformation Program ends. Over the remainder of the Lock In period, continue to provide support to help people master the future state they are now working in.

If you ask your learning and development professionals to implement a traditional training program, with the usual checkboxes and sign-offs, then that is what they will do. If you present the goal as immersion, your best learning and development professionals will be invigorated by the opportunity. They will design activities and communications accordingly, so people are able to learn to live and breathe the new world as rapidly as possible. And let us not forget, the faster an organization absorbs and masters the new world, the faster the business value of the transformation will be realized. So what will it be, box checking or immersion?

WHY DOES EVERYONE SUDDENLY LOVE THE OLD SYSTEM?

As you near the end of the program, it may surprise you to hear people waxing poetic about the old days. They may, much to your shock, suddenly speak fondly of the systems they have been complaining about for years. You may also notice an increase in people recounting heroic efforts of years past, that were undertaken to compensate for inefficient processes or unclear roles. You may find this perplexing. What is going on here? Should you worry?

Unless you have failed to deliver on the promises of your program, and these stories are intended to point out major flaws in your new world, there is nothing to worry about. This is an indication that people are mentally adapting to the new reality. Although the old ways are still comfortable, after a long period of uncertainty, people are seeing the new ways come to life. They are beginning to believe that change is really happening, that the new world is truly imminent. This manifests in an increase in stories told about "the good old days." View it as a sign that the old ways are beginning to transform into fond memories.

Engaging Your Secret Weapon

Hidden within your loyal employee base lies your secret weapon, just waiting to be engaged. These are people, concealed within your long-tenured employees, with unsung powers. These employees are often overlooked, dismissed out of hand, and viewed as part of the problem, driving the need to transform. Sometimes they are referred to as the "old guard," implying that they will defend the past. But that is an unfortunate generalization. There are people here who can be a powerful part of the solution. People who not only can change, but can become role models and agents of change during your transformation. You certainly do not want to dismiss them. Overlooking them would be a mistake. A missed opportunity. And, if you ask them, they aren't hidden at all.

To locate your secret weapons, search among your long-tenured employees for the team players with great attitudes. You know the

ones I'm talking about. The solid, reliable performers who show up every day. Upbeat. Always willing to help others. These are people who feel a strong pride in their organization and genuinely want to see it succeed. They may have been with the company for twenty, thirty, or even forty years, and these people are your secret weapon. They are easy to find, once you know what you are looking for.

Identify these people early, and choose some to be heavily involved in the transformation. Get them on board early in the program, educate them, and engage them in the communications and change management activities. As they help execute those activities, they will provide great insights along the way. Because they are heavily networked into the people system, they will know how people are feeling and where employees are confused or struggling. They will be able to assess if your proposed communications will resonate. They will provide valuable intel. Even more valuable, however, will be the example they set as they support the transformation, help others through the changes, and visibly walk the talk. What they demonstrate, quite simply and powerfully, is "If I can change, so can you."

Find these long-tenured employees—your secret weapons—and train them to be ambassadors for the new world. They will demonstrate to other employees that you do not have to be fresh out of school to adapt or to appreciate the need for change. The messages they send will be some of the most powerful ones in your arsenal for change, reducing anxiety and increasing engagement in those most entrenched in the old ways. These individuals will set themselves up as examples to dispel fear by acknowledging what others are thinking and feeling, and making things seem possible:

> "Yes, it's new. It's different. But look, I've learned it. If I can learn it, so can you."

> "It will be OK, it's not as scary as it appears."

> "We have a good set of immersive training experiences—I was part of creating them."

They are also excellent at encouraging others to see the value in the transformation, in a way that connects to them:

> "This is important to our future."

> "We haven't worked here this long just to let things fall apart now."

> "We've changed before, we can do it again."

> "Let's leave a great legacy."

It is also important to note that secret weapons love putting on their capes. Capes are, in fact, one of their favorite accessories. Speaking of which, let's lock this transformation in the right way . . .

A Superpowered Future State

Now, where did you leave your cape?

People are working through a lot of unknowns right now, and they could really use something familiar. It's a good time to draw everyone's attention to something that is *not* changing. Something like your superpower, which you activated in phase 3 (see page 123) and mobilized to great effect in phase 4 (see page 161). It is time to work that superpower as never before, so your organization can live to fight another day. Don't forget your cape!

As we've discussed, during this time of extreme change, people are naturally seeking comfort, searching for something familiar and genuine to ground them. This is why they try to use old processes, cling to old tools, and continue to follow old cultural norms. To lock in your business value, it is important to understand this, acknowledge that need for something familiar, and supply it where you can. Your superpower—that shared purpose or belief that makes your organization special—is that familiar something. It forms the connective tissue stretching from past to future, bridging the old world to the new.

Right now, immersion activities are underway and dispelling fear, continually making the future more known. Strategically incorporating your superpower within that immersion has a synergistic effect. Immersion is bringing the future closer. Meanwhile, your superpower is amplifying the connection to an enduring part of the past. The power move is to bring these together whenever possible.

During the insurance transformation I shared during Recon, we—myself and my Transformation team—leaned heavily on our organization's superpower to lock in that transformation. That organization's superpower was an obsession with taking care of customers, of doing right by them. It had a powerful legacy and had survived many decades. You could hear it in employees' stories— how when a customer's claim was uncertain, they were able to talk it through and find a way to say "yes" to approve it. Employees took a great deal of pride in this, in knowing that they would always do right by the customer.

While conducting the Transformation Program, we learned much about the particular language of this superpower and the different ways it manifested. To help lock in our transformation, we applied everything we had learned. That superpower was incorporated into communications and immersion activities, taking advantage of every available opportunity to point out where the new world would help employees do right by the customer. How the increased flexibility in a new process offered a claims agent the ability to better respond to a customer's needs. How customer service specialists, when using their new system properly, could rapidly pull up the customer information as they answered a call, saving the customer time on the phone. Every opportunity was taken to connect their superpower to actions and behaviors that would maximize the value of the new world.

By this point, you know the superpower language that resonates best with different groups in your organization. Thoughtfully embed your superpower within your communications throughout the Lock In phase. Build it into the immersion activities. Arm your secret weapons with it—they'll know how to best share it to help people through the changes. Remind people of their superpower. Make sure it stays true. Protect it. Nurture it. And let it lift you into the future.

Monitoring Vital Signs

How do you know when you're done?

By now, you know that Lock It In extends beyond the end of the Transformation Program. But for how long? The characteristics of your unique transformation will dictate the actual length. For a multiyear effort, it would not be surprising to begin Lock It In four to six months prior to the end of the Transformation Program, and extend it six to eight months thereafter, for a total length of roughly twelve months during which you immerse and monitor the organization. Generally speaking, the more you are transforming the underlying core culture of the organization, the longer it will take to cement. You do not need to decide the precise length up front. After the program concludes, I recommend deciding month by month whether to continue monitoring, based on your results. If you have effectively designed your immersion and monitoring, the cost of extending activities an extra few months should be minimal. And the payback significant.

Your organizational change management team built out a plan during the Transformation Program that is now being executed. That's a great start, but let's be honest. It is impossible to know in advance precisely how much immersion and repetition each employee will need. After all, this is entirely new. Therefore, as you lock it in, it is essential to monitor how well people are absorbing your future state.

Tests and surveys are obvious ways to gauge the absorption level, but before you allow them to be implemented, let's make sure they are being deployed for maximum value. This can be so much more than just a monitoring activity. With a little more effort and the right design, you can positively impact the people system while measuring it. In other words, we can monitor vital signs in such a way that it simultaneously increases employee motivation and engagement in the transformation journey. As you can see depicted below, there are five vital signs we want to monitor:

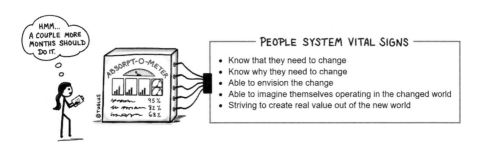

These are the things we want to be able to measure at various points throughout the Lock In period. Let's discuss three ways to monitor these vital signs: testing, competition, and surveying.

TESTING

Testing explores how well people are absorbing the mechanics of the future state. Tests could, of course, be administered in a standard, one-size-fits-all way. Let's not do that. I recommend they be conducted in a way that puts employees in control and encourages them to learn quickly. Put them in control by letting them test themselves as often as they want with on-demand testing. Furthermore, allow them to test out of any topic once they have mastered it, so they do not need to take any more classes on the topic.

This will motivate many employees to learn as quickly as possible. A series of such tests, conducted in conjunction with immersion activities, should lead up to program launch and beyond. These tests will also serve as a great tool later, post-transformation, for ongoing operations to onboard new employees and provide refresher courses. Deploying on-demand modules and tracking achievement is easy. Using these tools in a thoughtful manner can increase the very absorption that is being measured.

COMPETITION

Competitions can also motivate employees to master the future state with speed. They can be conducted in a way that naturally encourages employees to help each other master the new world, as long as you pit *teams* of employees against each other, not individuals. Allow them to compete for high average scores, completion dates, and ideas to increase the business value potential of the new world. This will tap into the competitive spirit of employees in a way that motivates them to help their teammates. And it will accelerate the attainment of business value.

SURVEYING

Surveys can share how employees feel and how well they understand what the future state entails. Design surveys based upon the five vital signs. Include questions such as "Do you understand the changes to your job?" and "How comfortable are you performing your new role?" Expect your first surveys to come back with very low marks. Now you have your baseline, and you know where you are starting from. From there you can really assess how well the future state is being locked in, and can adapt and accelerate immersion activities as necessary.

Deliver surveys regularly throughout the Lock In phase. The frequency with which you conduct them will greatly depend upon your type of transformation and is likely to vary over time. For instance, you might begin five months prior to program launch, sending out a survey every month, then as you near the launch date, shift to weekly surveys, and then back to monthly a few weeks after launch. Consider the schedules of your planned communications (from both the program team *and* your secret weapons) and immersion activities, and their expected impact on absorption of the new world. Map out how quickly you expect employees to reach various levels of comfort, knowledge, and capability. With that in mind, design your survey timing to correlate, but then adjust as needed along the way, adding more survey points as you need them.

Like frequency, how long you continue to distribute the surveys also depends on your unique transformation. While systems and processes can be mastered relatively quickly, culture change takes far longer to absorb. Meaningful progress in culture change can be seen six months after program launch, but realistically it takes at least a year in most cases for a new culture to fully soak in across the organization to the point where it is self-sustaining.

Once it does soak in, it will be obvious. You will hear employees—and leaders—consistently and matter-of-factly using the new language and exhibiting the new behaviors. I will always remember passing employees in the hallway about a year after our transformation to a culture of innovation (which I mentioned in the Recon report, see page 130). I overheard them casually chatting about the ideas and teams they were pulling together for the next innovation competition. It was being discussed in an upbeat, matter-of-fact way, the tone and conversation clearly demonstrating that the culture had sunk in: "Yep, I've already formed my team. I came up with an idea while testing out a new customer support process. Who's on your team? What's your idea? Or are you keeping it secret?" What was unspoken was also clear: *Of course we're assembling a team, of course we have innovative ideas, of course you will be assembling a team, this is something we do, we are an innovative organization.*

Pitfall Advisory #10: Abrupt Handoff

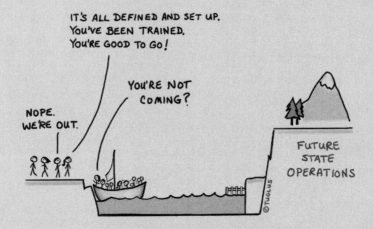

Welcome to the Abrupt Handoff pitfall, where ownership goes to die. (Overly dramatic? Just wait.)

The program team has been on a long, intense road. They're exhausted. They rush around, completing the multitude of last-minute execution details. The leaders who will inherit the future state are identified. A set of transitional meetings occurs. As the Transformation Program concludes, the program team hands off all of the product outputs by the program—the products, branding, software, tools, processes, definitions, and so on. Together with the new leaders, they check off a list of transition activities, one by one. They reach the end of the list. Done! The program team disbands.

Success is claimed. Time to celebrate! You're finished, right? Not so fast.

The leaders who have inherited this new world do not feel true ownership for it. They take control and technically *have* ownership, but they do not truly *feel* it. They do not feel accountable to achieve the promises made. They do not possess the drive and determination that are essential to nurture the potential and maximize the business value of this new world. And let's be fair—how would they? They barely understand the future state themselves. They are still learning. They are not certain they can achieve the promises that were made. So why would they commit to achieving value they fear is not possible?

You can try to impose accountability. Making the new leaders accountable for the transformation goals will certainly help. But do not be surprised to see this chipped away over time, through a series of perfectly reasonable rationalizations, causing a slow but steady erosion of the amount of value actually committed to—and therefore actually achieved. Much of their employee base will happily support this decrease in commitment. Even with immersion, their superpower, and the support of secret weapons, employees are still mastering this new world. They, too, are not absolutely confident in what can be achieved.

A set of well-intended meetings was conducted with the inheriting leaders to work through the transition, but it just wasn't enough. Something more dramatic must be done. Ownership for realizing the potential of this future state must be secured at the leadership level. The amount of work and energy that has been expended to get to this point is substantial. Threats in the outside world are looming. There is an urgent need to deliver meaningful business value. Let's catapult over this destructive pitfall. It's time for a heart transplant.

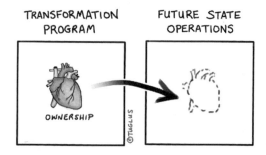

Executing a Heart Transplant to Secure Ownership

We need to cement this transformation. The immersion program is underway. Secret weapons have been engaged. Your superpower is front and center. Monitoring has been put in place. But it's not enough. It is time to execute a heart transplant. I'm not talking about remote surgery with robots and virtual reality. I am talking about ownership—the heart of your Transformation team. A heart transplant will migrate ownership at the leadership level.

During Recon and the Transformation Program, a fledgling sense of ownership has formed across the organization. Ensuring this sense of ownership stays alive, and thrives, is critical to the realization of your business value. With the right moves, you will be able to leap right over that Abrupt Handoff pitfall.

Remember that top talent we placed on the Transformation team? You have probably forgotten what they used to do and where they came from, back in the days before Recon and the Transformation Program. For the past few years, these talented individuals have lived and breathed this transformation and the promises it holds. They have gained invaluable cross-functional insights. Developed new skills. Stretched themselves further than they ever expected. Grown confidence in their ability to tackle any challenge. And delivered something great that has never before been done at this organization. They have *owned* it. And guess what? They know exactly what the new world should look like, what it is intended to accomplish, and how it can be achieved. And they feel a deep, unrelenting sense of ownership for seeing it live and thrive.

It is time to execute a heart transplant by taking these individuals, who possess this amazing sense of ownership, and moving them back into the business. Place them into key roles in the new organization, into the most important transformational business areas. Director of customer service. Senior director of claims. Head of data management and business intelligence. Head of product delivery. Leading the establishment of a new business. These are just some of the roles I have placed such individuals into. This is how you will transfer ownership from the program team to ongoing business teams. This is your final move to lock in the business value and realize the potential of your Transformation Program. Think about it. What are the most important roles in your new world?

Are you locked in? It is possible to successfully execute the first four phases of the transformation journey, only to tragically discover that in the end much of the business value was left unrealized. This happens surprisingly easily. Even though the activities in Lock It In are straightforward, this phase requires energy, determination, and perseverance at a time when energy is low, ownership is changing hands, and often all of the allocated funding has been spent. Many organizations fall prey to the Abrupt Handoff and do not realize they lost business value until much later. If ever. The changing of personnel over time obscures the memory of the original potential, and leadership doesn't even know what they've lost.

Fortunately, there are a number of tools at your disposal to help lock in value: immersion, your secret weapon, your superpower, a heart transplant. If you are serious about realizing the potential of your transformation, the journey is not truly over until you Lock It In.

You know what to do. You know how critical this is. And you're serious about business value. You can do this. Lock it in.

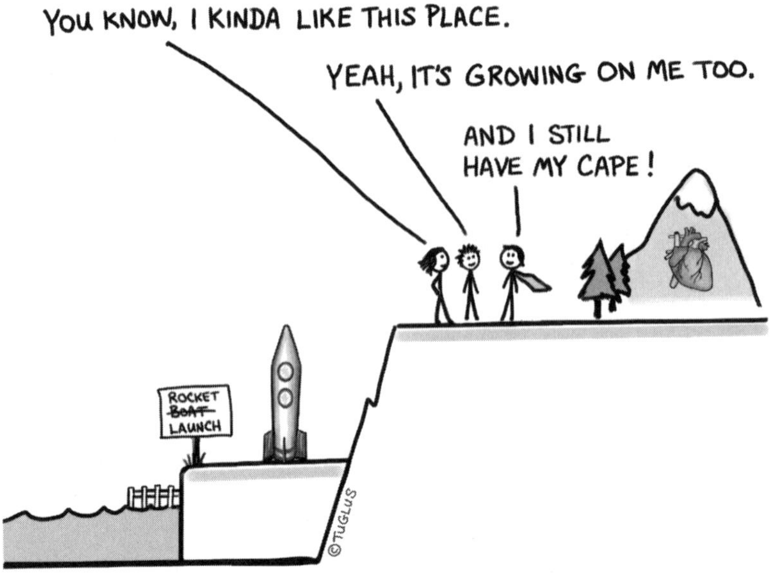
YOU KNOW, I KINDA LIKE THIS PLACE.
YEAH, IT'S GROWING ON ME TOO.
AND I STILL HAVE MY CAPE!
ROCKET BOAT LAUNCH
©TUGLUS

Conclusion

YOU HAVE SUCCESSFULLY launched and landed many, many ships. Triumphed over diverse challenges. Turbulent seas. Dangerous dragons. And the most intimidating challenge of all—human nature itself. You have emerged, battle-weary but victorious. Your death-defying feats have beaten the odds. What were the secrets to success?

A transformation is a perilous journey, and you took it seriously—conducting the proper advance education and preparation, and executing all phases with the rigor and intensity they deserve. Because securing the right know-how and maintaining commitment throughout the journey was essential, you invested in the right talent and actively cultivated commitment. All of this created a reinforcing effect throughout the journey, benefiting later phases. Living the laws of transformation, you kept people at the heart of it all and led them through the journey in ways that dispelled fear, tapped into their superpower, and kept them engaged. You conducted activities with urgency, successfully combatting organizational fatigue, while keeping an eye on the ever-advancing world.

While vaulting across ten treacherous pitfalls and defeating dragons, you kept the achievement of business value front and center. As the Transformation Program concluded, you did not falter, exhibiting great determination to complete the full journey and lock in the value. It wasn't easy, but you persevered. Real business benefits were delivered. And do you ever have an epic tale to tell.

While celebrating your organization's achievements, you may notice that while you have leapfrogged over the competition and harnessed disruption for now, the world is *still* moving. Rapidly. And you have a nagging suspicion that someday you will find yourself in the same position that you were in at the beginning of this journey: on the precipice of a transformation.

Some leaders say that transformation never ends. That organizations should constantly be transforming. How do you feel about that? Overwhelmed? Exhausted? I'm with you. While this is a technically accurate, logical conclusion, the notion is disheartening.

Yes, the world is constantly changing and you should likely be planning your next transformation as you complete this one. But the statement, "transformation never ends" implies a constant churn that is, quite frankly, exhausting to even think about. Consequently, conveying this sentiment to your employees will immediately trigger fear and resistance. Do not do this.

At the end of a long, perilous journey, there must be closure. People—both leaders and employees—must feel a sense of accomplishment. A sense of completion. The reality of human nature is that we cannot operate continuously with high intensity and urgency. Organizations are people. We are not robots, no matter how digital our lives have become. Sure, we've developed a number of cyborg appendages to extend our abilities. But at the heart, organizations are a system of people. We fear the unknown. We need relativity. We want to be part of something great. And until enough disruption can be imagined, and someone can make it obvious just how much our organization can—or must—change, until someone can show us how it is possible, we simply cannot see it. We cannot imagine it happening. And therefore, cannot generate the willingness to achieve it. Consequently, I believe that transformation most naturally occurs in spurts and that it will continue to do so. Otherwise your organization will be fatigued before you even begin. So don't beat yourself up for not starting this sooner. But once you have decided to embark upon a transformation, then take it seriously. Commit to doing it right. Or don't bother doing it at all.

And at the end of a transformation, make sure your people feel that it has concluded. That though they will continue to build mastery in this new world, this is the new current state. Not forever, but for a while. Long enough to rest up for the next big challenge.

While they are doing that, help them look back and see the journey from which they have emerged for the epic tale that it is. This is the final evolution of your transformation's story. With the Transformation Story as a base, build in the amazing stories of how teams came together to make this new world possible. How business value was threatened many, many times, but they persevered, determined to make it possible. How they leapt over pitfalls in death-defying feats of business transformation. How they *owned* this.

Telling the tale is a great way to celebrate the completion of the transformation journey. You have triumphed, vaulting over perilous pitfalls, accomplishing something both rare and mission critical. There is an amazing tale to be told. Encourage the organization to tell their epic tale for closure, for celebration, and so that others may learn from them. This goes for not only the transformation leader and team leads, but for all the employees who went on the journey. This is not so much *your* story as it is *their* story. The tale should be told to new hires. At retirement parties, when your secret weapons retire. At conferences. Speaking of which, remember those outsiders, convinced that you couldn't hack it? Guess whose conference presentation they won't be missing?

When I was transforming the product line I talked about earlier—the one that produced the majority of the organization's revenue—our situation was well known across the industry. The current state

Now, granted, we were the former subsidiary of a hundred-year-old company. But remember: any organization can transform with the right know-how and commitment.

product line was branded with our former parent company's name, General Motors, and our contract had a widely known expiration date. Our situation was made even more obvious as GM put out for bid, then launched, a set of directly competing products through a different provider. All of our competitors knew the precise date at which we could no longer sell these products, and they knew almost exactly how much we depended upon them.

Furthermore, many former employees were now at those competitors and were well versed in our legacy culture. They assumed we would slowly fade into obscurity, that all of our customers would move to competing products as our end date arrived. When we saw them at conferences, they laughed at us. But worse than that were the matter-of-fact statements. While some may have only been hoping, I believe many of these people were genuinely convinced that we would not get our act together, that we just couldn't compete. Now, granted, we *were* the former subsidiary of a hundred-year-old company. But remember: any organization can transform with the right know-how and commitment.

As we launched the new product line, we persuaded the vast majority of our existing distribution partners—and some new ones—to migrate to our new product and experience. In fact, we exceeded our forecasts. It was remarkably successful. Can you imagine how employees felt the next time they saw all those naysayers? The next time one of their friends, now working for a competitor, called them up to chat? From operations to sales, they had all been part of something great and they had an amazing tale to tell. It was told at conferences, it was told to new hires, it was celebrated and shared far and wide. Because it was pretty epic.

A transformation is an important time in the history of your organization. You are at the precipice of something—a new market direction, a new operating approach, a new culture, a new world. In order to achieve it, you must be able to imagine it. To almost taste it. Then, in order to turn that concept into reality, you need true transformation know-how and commitment. With this, you are able to lead people on a journey to a new land to deliver an amazing future.

Business transformation is complex, multifaceted, fraught with peril, and in many cases, death-defying. But it is absolutely possible.

THIS PIT LOOKS POPULAR.

©TUGLUS

Search and Rescue
An Assessment Tool for Transformations in Trouble

AS YOU KNOW, transformation is a perilous journey. There are many ways to become diverted by a dragon or stuck in a pit. Given the high failure rate (70 percent according to McKinsey[4]), at some point in your career, you will almost certainly encounter a transformation in trouble. Perhaps more than once.

Trying to understand what is really going on inside a troubled transformation can leave you confused and overwhelmed. Most executives will hire someone to handle that. But if you're like me, you like to know how things work. You like to peer under the cover, to

---

[4] McKinsey & Company. "The 'How' of Transformation." Last updated May 9, 2016. https://www.mckinsey.com/industries/retail/our-insights/the-how-of-transformation.

look inside a system to see the fundamental drivers, to learn the core essence. And—regardless of whether you *like* to do that—if you are hiring someone to investigate, perhaps you should understand what you are hiring them to do. That would be smart—otherwise, how will you be able to set clear expectations and receive actionable outputs? You *are*, after all, the owner of those outputs. Even if consultants produce them. (You can't outsource ownership.) This short guide, based on my extensive transformation experience, is designed to help you investigate a troubled transformation.

A failing transformation is most visible during the Transformation Program phase. For the purposes of this guide, let's assume that you have walked in while the Transformation Program is underway. Maybe you're new to the organization. Maybe you're the CEO and you've been too trusting; perhaps you hired (or appointed) the wrong leader or allowed another executive team member to hire the wrong leader. Regardless of how you got there, there is a Transformation Program that now has your attention. And it is worrisome.

The program feels... troubled. Or perhaps it is you who are troubled. The overarching intent of the effort seems right (though you aren't absolutely certain), but the program itself feels off. You just can't seem to develop confidence in the initiative. It is difficult to determine whether the program is unhealthy or misguided, or if it's just your lack of familiarity that makes you uncomfortable. What you do know, however, is that the more questions you ask, the more questions you have.

You're getting surface-level answers to your questions, and the gossip is not good. Now, you wouldn't make important decisions based on gossip, right? Of course not. It's just one data point. Some members of your executive team are suggesting that the program will not deliver. Or that it is just not worth continuing. They have better things that you could spend that money on, they tell you. Are these political maneuvers? Are they just testing you? Are these executives the ones that need to be coached, that must be pushed to get on board and support the program? Or is there truly something wrong here? One thing is for certain—you need to find out.

If this transformation is mission critical and not on track to deliver, then you should be very concerned, because your organization is running out of time. The world continues to move forward and organizational fatigue is threatening to set in (as discussed in the fourth law of transformation on page 39). These are not forces to be trifled with. Additionally, time and money are being spent on this program. Every month. The meter is running. I suspect you have already asked finance for the monthly run rate, so you know exactly what this is costing.

Transformation Programs in motion tend to stay in motion, long after they should have been halted or redesigned.

This urgently requires investigation. You need to rapidly perform a Search and Rescue operation, to determine if there is indeed trouble, identify the most relevant underlying issues, and then if necessary (and viable), devise a rescue plan. To be clear, you are not replacing the leader and replanning the entire effort. Not yet. Not until you know more. In fact, you might not need to do that at all. Right now, you just want to know if your suspicions are correct.

Assessing a Transformation Program appears easy at first. Interview some people, attend some meetings, and you will easily notice a number of things that could be improved. But knowing which of those things truly matters, diagnosing the fundamental issues they may be masking, and determining what to do about it—well, that is all actually quite difficult. Transformation Programs in motion tend to stay in motion, long after they should have been halted or redesigned. One of the most common reasons for this is the difficulty in assessing one in process. So let's demystify that. Let's pull off the cover and delve inside a Transformation Program to inspect the most critical components.

Transformations exist to deliver business value. You have learned that, at the core, transformations fail because people either do not know how to transform or are not truly committed. Or both (see page 7). There are many other elements to a successful transformation, but

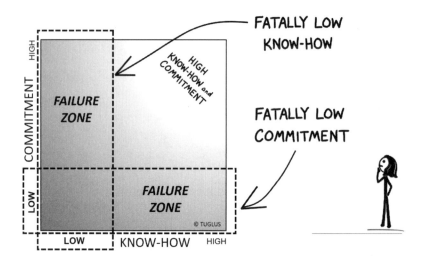

FATALLY LOW
KNOW-HOW

FAILURE
ZONE

HIGH
KNOW-HOW and
COMMITMENT

FATALLY LOW
COMMITMENT

FAILURE
ZONE

© TUGLUS

COMMITMENT — HIGH / LOW

LOW / KNOW-HOW / HIGH

these must be at the center. If both are not maintained at healthy levels throughout every phase of the journey, your transformation *will* fail. These critical components—know-how, commitment, and, of course, business value—are what we will focus our Search efforts around. By the end of our Search effort, we will have a good idea of whether we believe this transformation will produce a desirable output based on these factors. Transformation team members may be lost, languishing in pits, or diverted by dragons. Let's find out where they're at (Search), and then devise a rescue strategy (Rescue). During Search, there are four questions to answer:

- **Business value potential:** Is there really a point to this?

- **Commitment:** Is the organization (the leadership) serious?

- **Know-how:** Do they (the Transformation team and leadership) have the right know-how?

- **Business value achievement:** Will they really achieve value?

You can stop Search anytime. If at any point during the investigation, you've discovered some pretty serious issues and feel you've gathered enough information, then halt your Search efforts and move directly into a Rescue operation. Can the troubled transformation be rescued? What can be done? Rescue options will be discussed after the four Search questions are explored. The clock is ticking and the meter is running. Grab your magnifying glass and let's start the Search.

Search Part 1: Business Value Potential

Your organization entered into this transformation for a reason. In this first part of our Search, we want to decide if that reason was valid—if this transformation *ever* had a real chance to deliver material business value. Simply put, was this a good idea? A worthy endeavor? Or not?

This may feel like an unnecessary visit to the past. Does it really matter what the goals were, if the team isn't actually delivering on them? Good question. First of all, we don't know for certain—yet— that they are not delivering. Second, and more important, there is a greater concern here: Is there business value that must be achieved that is *vital* to the future and survival of this organization? Understanding the original intent will provide better insight into whether or not a transformation is still needed, and this will also put the program into context and ultimately inform your choice of Rescue activities.

WHAT WAS THE VISION?

Go back to the beginning to familiarize yourself with the original intent of the transformation. This material should exist somewhere. Perhaps not of the quality we'd prefer, but something should be documented. What is the original vision? What is the program intended to achieve? What advantage is the organization expecting to derive in the marketplace? Collect any documentation available like the following:

- Original vision statement

- Current state analysis

- Disruption analysis

Basically, we're looking for documented evidence that explains why this organization is doing this. What was it that convinced the leadership team to begin this transformation in the first place? Not why they *think* they are doing this, but documented evidence detailing why they *actually* set out on this journey. We want facts. We'll gather opinions later.

WAIT. WHAT IF THE VISION OR GOALS OF THE PROGRAM CHANGED AT SOME POINT?

If this program has officially changed its original goals and/or vision, then wherever I talk about the original intent, we also need to understand the current intent: What is the current vision? Is it different? If so, why? Conduct this first Search activity against *both* the current and original. Hunt down any additional documentation that explains the changes to the vision or goals. Conduct interviews as necessary. If the goals of this program materially changed more than once, gather as much information as you can regarding all the changes.

You may be tempted to only assess the current goals. Don't do that. The original goals and vision may point to something critically needed by the organization—if so, you want to know.

WAS THE VISION IMPAIRED BY PITFALLS?

Take a close look at the documents you have collected and conduct a pitfall check. Did the transformation get stuck in one or more of the common Preparation pitfalls (starting on page 64) that tend to impair vision?

- **The Allure of Benchmarking:** Did they set the transformation goal of achieving parity with the current benchmark for their industry?

- **Just Technology, Please:** Did their vision focus purely on technology replacement?

- **Technology as a Magic Process Fix:** Did their vision assume technology alone would deliver meaningful process change?

- **Centralize It All:** Did they blindly plan to centralize?

If the team fell into any of these pitfalls—maybe they are even still in one today—the Transformation Program is heading toward weak goals. You must take a close look at whether those goals are worth achieving as they stand. If they do not impress you, then you may decide to stop the Search work here and shift directly into Rescue mode. If you believe they are worthwhile, continue forward.

WERE THE GOALS CLEAR?

After checking for common Preparation pitfalls, it's time to take a closer look at the specific goals that were set for the future state before the Transformation Program. Did the team conduct a Reconnaissance Mission or something similar? We're looking for a clear definition of the mid-level future state goals, with specific numbers and outcomes, clear enough to map a route to the future. Did the Transformation team rush off into a program, skipping Recon altogether, and fall into the Too Deep, Too Soon pitfall (see page 97)?

Hunt down any documentation of the mid-level goals, what work was done to support those goals, and the story that was told to convince leadership that the goals made sense. Seek out this information regarding the original goals (and current goals, if they differ):

- The Transformation Story (see page 135), or any similar material, such as pitch decks or business case documentation, that explains the case for change, and the goals of the transformation

- Any material that fed into that story or case, providing supporting evidence for the story

- Initial estimates of program-related costs and benefits, especially those committed and formalized in the business plan

- Current goals for the transformation (if they differ from original)

Review all of this material to develop a sense of the originally envisioned business outcomes. Did the organization really know what it was setting out to achieve in a Transformation Program? Were clear, tangible mid-level business goals set? Why was commitment granted to execute this program? What information was provided? Did the organization execute the right type of work to justify approval? Did the goals change at some point? Are those clear? Or is the team still running toward a fuzzy future?

If goals are ambiguous, it will be impossible to know if the program is achieving the desired business value. We may have found the root cause (or one of them) of the current troubled situation. You may choose to head directly into Rescue mode right now. If the goals seem solid, continue forward to search for other issues.

ARE THE CURRENT GOALS STILL RELEVANT?

Suppose the goals are clear. Or, at least they were when they were set (or revised). Now think about these goals. Sitting where the organization does today, does this program still make sense?

The world has been moving. Take into consideration the broader context of the world you are in right now—do these transformation goals still hold? Typically, the case for your transformation will still hold. But sometimes, it does not. Maybe it was never truly worthy in the first place. Or it was only worthy if it completed much faster and cost a lot less than what is now projected. Sometimes, external events have occurred that require adjustments to be made to the goals. And sometimes, stakeholders see those external forces and begin to believe that this is no longer a worthy endeavor. And that directly impacts their commitment. Let's take a look at that in Search Part 2.

Search Part 2: Commitment

At this point you understand the intent of the program, believe that clear goals are being pursued, and have confirmed that they still make sense today. You have confirmed that this transformation has the *potential* to deliver meaningful business value. Now let's dig into the reality. The potential is there, but will the team be able to pull this off? We're talking about commitment and know-how. We'll begin with commitment. Does the Transformation Program have commitment? To investigate this, let's go see if everyone agrees on and

supports the transformation goals. In the first part of our investigation, we wanted the facts, and we hunted down documented evidence regarding the purpose of this transformation. Now we want opinions. Perceptions. What do key stakeholders *believe* is the purpose of the transformation? What do they *perceive* the program goals to be? And are they supportive?

IS THERE A SHARED UNDERSTANDING OF THE GOALS?

To get at those beliefs, perceptions, and support, it is necessary to conduct some interviews with key executives, Transformation team members, and other stakeholders. As you interview each person, note that person's understanding of the transformation goals and gauge their level of support for the initiative. Interviews like this tend to flow best when unstructured, so be sure to make it more a conversation than an interrogation. Ask questions such as the following:

· What is the current situation in the industry faced by the company?

· What are the greatest opportunities? Risks? Challenges?

· How will this transformation take advantage of those opportunities?

· How will this transformation mitigate those risks?

· What are the goals of this program?

· How important is the program?

- What benefits does your department, division, or function expect from this transformation?

- Where are those documented? Who can tell me more?

- How did you feel about the program when it was first introduced?

- What is your level of engagement in the program?

- What support has the program asked of you?

- How confident are you in the program?

After conducting the interviews, create a very simple table, like the one below. First write down, concisely, the goals that were unearthed in the first part of our investigation. Then, next to them, lay out the information you have just gathered regarding the perceptions of each stakeholder. If the program has pivoted, include an additional column for the current stated goals next to the original goals.

CURRENT GOALS	ORIGINAL GOALS	PERCEIVED GOALS						
		CEO	EXECUTIVE 1	EXECUTIVE 2	TRANSF. LEADER	PROGRAM LEAD A	PROGRAM LEAD B	...

Once it's complete, review the information you've gathered. Do perceived goals match the actual goals? Look for differing perceptions of the goals. Now create a second table (see page 212) to help you assess support from leadership. Based on the interviews, jot down your beliefs regarding the level of support from each leader. Did they seem engaged and knowledgeable? Committed to helping? Or distant and disengaged? Were they knowledgeable yet careful and cautious in how they speak about the program—in other words, not very supportive?

It is absolutely possible to find people who are quite knowledgeable about the program but who are not supporting it. Perhaps because they believe the program is a bad idea. Or because they do not believe it can be delivered. Or because they just don't believe in the team. Some of the most informative interviews will be with people who took the time to really understand the transformation and then chose to opt out.

SUPPORT and ENGAGEMENT

CEO	EXECUTIVE 1	EXECUTIVE 2	TRANSF. LEADER	PROGRAM LEAD A	PROGRAM LEAD B	...

As you review your charts, you may be thinking that this is going to get political. You're right, it probably will. But get the most honest information you can. Create a very candid version of the Support and Engagement chart for yourself, then decide how to summarize, organize, and formally communicate the information to others.

What have you learned? How aligned are people? More importantly, how aligned are their perceptions to the program's stated goals? If perceptions vary greatly, it may indicate poor communication by the Transformation team, which in turn suggests weak transformation know-how. Alternatively, it may reveal political turmoil: that stakeholders are trying to influence the goals and change them for personally beneficial reasons. This is especially common with the introduction of a new CEO, when leaders often actively push personal agendas.

It is also possible that something has changed out in the world, or elsewhere in the company, and that is putting pressure on the program. That external pressure has not yet been addressed by the program, and perceptions are changing because of it. Whatever the reason, if the executive team is not aligned and supportive—if they are not committed—it certainly does not bode well for transformation success.

ARE THERE MORE CLUES IN THE BUSINESS PLAN?

Another source of intelligence regarding commitment is the business plan, an organization's forecast of revenue streams and costs over time. Study the business plans of each business line that should experience a meaningful benefit from the completion of this Transformation Program. Were the originally anticipated program benefits built into their business plans? If not, then why?

Sometimes they won't be, because a company chooses to record the program benefits elsewhere. They may be inserted into the rollup of the business plans, into a higher level plan. But wherever the benefits were incorporated, find them and conduct some forensic analysis. First, acquire a copy of every version of the business plan from the point the program was approved. Now check for changes. Have transformation benefits quietly—or not so quietly—been removed from business plans over time?

This happens more often than you may think. The executives who were promised major benefits from the program do not want to be held accountable for the results. Either they were never truly committed or they no longer believe these results can be achieved. They are not willing to expend political capital to address this head-on, so they quietly remove some transformation benefit from their multiyear forecast every time it is updated. If this is happening, talk to them and try to get specific explanations for why they believe the goals will not be achieved. You want to determine if there is really an issue with the program here, or if this is just classic corporate executive self-protection in progress.

WHAT'S THE INCENTIVE HERE?

While we're thinking about politics, this is also a good time to check out the incentives of key leaders—the assigned transformation leader, the sponsor, and the executives expected to receive benefits. The transformation leader may not be truly committed to this transformation. Did they want this job? Do they have the background for it? Were they provided an experienced coach? They may not feel equipped to execute this. They may not have asked for this position. This happens.

Early in my career there were times that I was given the opportunity to lead a transformation not only because I had the know-how but also because it was the big, complex, global, cross-functional challenge that no one else wanted to take a career risk on. Score! But not everyone wants the job. And they do not always feel that they can turn it down. So they say yes, but their heart isn't in it.

What about the executive sponsor's incentive? If the executive sponsor is not the CEO, who is it? What are they most motivated by? Are they taking ownership of the initiative for the benefit (reputedly) of the entire organization? Or just for themselves? The executives who are expected to benefit most from the program, what do they care about? What is the incentive for each of them? It is not always obvious. A long-tenured executive may not have their heart in it. On the other hand, that person may be all in, wanting to leave a legacy. You can't assume; you must talk to them and assess for yourself.

COMMITMENT: WHAT'S THE VERDICT?

Lack of executive support is a famous transformation failure point. Executive support represents organizational commitment. And commitment is a critical component of success in any transformation. So what's the verdict? Do you have commitment? Through your interviews and analysis, you have formed an opinion: Is there real support for the program right now? Was there real commitment at the start? Did the team even have a chance?

If the program has fatally low commitment, it's not going to make it. Form an opinion regarding *why* commitment is lacking. This will greatly influence the Rescue actions you decide to invest in. Why doesn't it have commitment? There can be many reasons: external events, politics, outsourced ownership. Did the organization fall into the Outsourcing Ownership pitfall (see page 107)? If consultants were hired to handle the entirety of bridging the vision to the Transformation Program, there was limited commitment at the outset. It's possible the effort was funded but key leadership did not actually commit to supporting it. Yet another possible reason is that initial commitment was granted but the program team lacked the know-how to sustain it. So we'll dig into this team's know-how next.

Search Part 3: Know-How

Do you recall when we were discussing rocket ship operations (see page 164), and I said we would not be taking apart rockets? If you were disappointed, well, now's your chance. (Although, more accurately, we're dissecting the operations of the rocket transportation company, not the rockets. But I won't begrudge you a few rockets along the way.) By now you understand that both know-how and commitment are absolutely essential. We just assessed commitment, and now it is time for know-how.

Is this team inherently capable of delivering? Do the program leader and team possess the transformation know-how to execute and deliver such a complex and critical endeavor? Are they able to keep business value in focus throughout? Let's dive into the operations of this program to find out.

The investigation of know-how includes three assessments. We'll connect program activities to spending, study the general effectiveness of program leadership, and dig into risk management to see if this team really knows what they're doing. While we assess the operation, we want things to continue running as normally as possible. Know that the team will naturally be nervous and anxious, especially if the program is in trouble. We do not want to frighten anyone; we just want answers. People under pressure tend to behave less predictably, and we do not want our Search team to put the Transformation Program further in peril. Therefore, we will try to ask for relatively simple things that should be easy for the team to produce. That being said, if you are not getting a good sense of know-how from what you are provided, push further and go as deep as you need to. This is too important not to.

WHAT'S THE STORY BEHIND THE MONTHLY SPEND?

We will begin with something that should be easy to collect: program spending information. Get the numbers and map the monthly spend of the Transformation Program over time. Start the chart at the inception of the program and include data through to today. Make sure the spend is fully loaded with all program costs—do not forget to include the cost of all people time contributed. There are often costs left out of the official number, and that may require getting estimates of time contributed by a number of people, then estimating the cost and adding it in. It is common for costs to reside in multiple locations across the company, and we want an accurate representation of the true cost. Be prepared to face resistance and convoluted bookkeeping. Don't worry if you have to make some estimates.

Once you have mapped out the spend over time, conduct individual meetings with each of the Transformation Program leaders. Ask them to walk you through the story that lies behind the spending. What was happening each month? What activities were conducted? How many people were involved? What contracts were executed? Were tools purchased or subscribed to? Work products produced? And so on.

After the meetings, review your notes and spend chart. Consider what you heard. Does the spending ebb and flow in a logical way over time? You should expect to see certain patterns. Teams require ramp-up periods. Technology development and implementation, including large software efforts, should have heavy or light spending in predictable areas. Regulatory approval should require pockets of activity and waiting periods. Agencies often bill in concert with the delivery of their work products. Ongoing services and subscriptions will have predictable up-front costs and a logical time at which recurring costs begin.

Where does the spending and the story make sense together, and where does it not? Do we have any suspiciously steep slopes in spending, that do not logically connect to the activities occurring at the time? Remember the Too Deep, Too Soon pitfall (see page 97), where a team runs from their vision toward a detailed program, only to end up in the pit? Falling into that pit often produces an unnaturally steep slope in spending. Look for abnormalities like that. Also, thinking about what you were told, consider whether the order of the activities made sense operationally. Document your thoughts and conduct follow-up meetings as needed.

ARE THERE CLUES TO KNOW-HOW IN STATUS ROUTINES?

To further assess the know-how of program leadership, look at the program's status routines. There should be easily accessible documents, produced by regular program communications and meetings. Using this information, our primary goal is to get a sense of the team's ability to think systemically, orchestrate people and activities, and anticipate issues.

Pull the past six to nine months of status updates and executive communications. These may exist in multiple forms: status reports, newsletters, meeting minutes, presentations, videos.

Study them, looking for patterns. Try to follow the commitments and achievements. Is it clear what is being committed and tracked? Or does it seem deliberately ambiguous? Allowing teams to march toward fuzzy goals and make unclear commitments is a sign of weak leadership. Is everything always rosy-sounding? Is there accountability and follow-up for items promised in past status reports? Experienced transformation leaders want to hear the reality of the situation and will hold people accountable for their commitments. Such leaders are also quite good at anticipating issues that may emerge and harm the program, so look for clues regarding how issues are handled. Do issues seem to suddenly appear out of nowhere? If so, is it because the team is genuinely surprised? Or deliberately not communicating them?

You may not be able to tell much from reviewing the artifacts, especially if this program is in trouble. So it will be necessary to go further and attend some meetings. You will learn a lot here if you know what to look for. Start with some regular status meetings and program leadership meetings. Is the program team leading or just coordinating? Are they anticipating issues or reacting? Are they flustered by challenges or invigorated? Consider the types of discussions that occur. Do they understand that their jobs are not only to deliver the activities, but also to shape the people system? Do people feel engaged in making this a success?

Also attend at least one set of regular stakeholder meetings. There may be a steering committee. Or a governance committee. Or both. Or a key stakeholder meeting with another name entirely. Visit them all. Note the kind of conversation that is occurring. Watch body language and listen to the tone of voices. Is the program team leading or just coordinating? Are they engaging the stakeholders in a productive way? Do people feel engaged in making this a success? You will also learn more about commitment in these meetings, so be sure to jot down any additional observations for that as well.

As you attend meetings, it will be quite beneficial to review the culture of transformation (see page 148) and the characteristics of a great transformation leader (see page 78). How does this Transformation team compare? Record your notes and let's conduct one more review to complete our assessment of transformation know-how. This one will be fun. We'll be searching for the risk cauldron (see page 20).

ASSESS RISK MANAGEMENT

Risk management should be a natural part of the transformation culture. Unfortunately, all too often I find well-meaning people

implementing awkward, non-value-added routines as a substitute for real risk management. Don't be fooled by process rigor or formality. In some cases, risk management will be very regimented and formal—this is not uncommon when expensive, complex tools are being built. In other cases, it may be less so, as in a transformation that is exclusively about culture change. Sometimes it may never even be officially referred to as risk management. We do not care about process rigor or labels. We care about mindset. Any discussion of risks should be about keeping the program moving toward business value as quickly and surely as possible. Similarly, we do not care about quantity—the number of risks on a list is irrelevant; a big cauldron is still just a cauldron.

An assessment of risk management can be more art than science, so our work here will require you to really put some thought into it. Acquire the risk logs—the full logs as well as the versions that are brought to executive updates. Review the past three to six months (more if they are only updated quarterly). We want to determine if risk management is a natural part of the team's program thinking. Are risks well thought out, and are they (for the most part) actionable to mitigate? (There will always be some risks with no possible actions other than monitoring.) Look over the risks. Are the things listed worth talking about? A very simple approach is to ask the following question of yourself as you look at each risk: "As it is written, is the monitoring, tracking, and discussion of this risk worthwhile? Or is it a waste of time?"

Suppose you see a risk like this: "The world could change and the program is no longer needed." True but useless. Check the "waste of time" box. It is a waste of time to write down, track, and discuss this risk. It is too broad. It is always possible for any program. It is neither well thought out nor specific enough to do anything with. Throw it back into the cauldron (if you see that risk, you know there's a cauldron around here somewhere).

If you discover a recurrence of "waste of time" risks, you have a problem. You want to see a logical, value-minded assessment of things that could prevent transformation success. You want to see thoughtful and precise items such as "a change in interest rates of more than two basis points would negate the business value of workstream 3." Now that is clear. The team can monitor that and create plans around it. Another example: "the procurement contract for the robots took two weeks longer than planned, putting the robot launch date at risk by two weeks." Again, that is nice and clear. Actions can be taken to mitigate that, and downstream effects can be measured and managed.

Speaking of actions, choose some of the risks—some of the good ones, based on the criteria we just discussed—and follow up on how they were handled. Talk to the program leaders and the owners of the risks to learn how they approached mitigation. Assess whether the real risks are being taken seriously, keeping in mind that sometimes there is no reasonable mitigation possible.

The bottom line is that risks should be thoughtfully identified, well managed, and logically communicated as a natural part of the program execution. If the team is not incorporating this mindset, or just seems to be going through the motions, treat it as a red flag. This signals weak transformation know-how.

At this point, you have a good sense of the Transformation team's capabilities and have developed an opinion regarding their level of transformation know-how. Suppose you have uncovered a few concerning things. You might feel tempted to continue this know-how investigation and dig deeper into program operations to try to find everything that you can. That would be lengthy and unnecessary for our purposes. We're not doing that. We are executing a surgical strike into targeted areas and getting out fast. If you're convinced they lack the know-how, shift into Rescue mode.

If you have developed confidence in the team's core transformation know-how, proceed to the final part of our Search investigation.

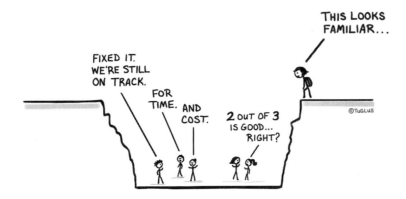

Search Part 4: Business Value Achievement

Is business value truly being achieved? If the results of the assessment thus far indicate serious issues, you are unlikely to find out. There might be some value buried in there, but you'll need an excavator. And if the program is in its infancy, this fourth Search investigation is not worth attempting. It is only later, when there are enough completed activities to dig into, that you can find valuable information.

Even if enough of the transformation has been executed and things are pretty good, getting a real answer to this question isn't easy and will involve going deep into program activities. If you're up for that, here are some ways to go about it:

Change control documentation: Review the change control logs and meeting minutes for clues to reductions in business value. This presumes the team is logging scope decreases as well as increases. If you can identify things that were removed from scope along the way, but seem important, investigate those further through interviews.

Trade-off investigation: Interview key business owners. Conduct discussions regarding trade-offs that have been made relating to business value. Start by asking about the original business outcomes that were expected from the activities they care about most. Then ask them to walk you through all the challenges, tough decisions, and trade-offs they have been engaged in throughout the program. What happened when things got tough? When timelines got tight? When dependencies weren't ready in time? When cost estimates came in dramatically higher for an activity? When push came to shove, what was sacrificed? Listen carefully for a pattern. Is business value continually sacrificed to meet time and budget commitments? Also, were these people included in all the decisions to cut their business value?

Activity deep dive: Choose a couple of the program goals that you are most concerned about. Identify the associated program activities. Choose roughly five activities for your sample, in different areas. The best ones will have clearly designated future state owners. To assess if the value of those activities is really being delivered, interview those owners as well as the program team members who are executing the work.

Is real value being created? How the activity is implemented has a lot of bearing on the ultimate value derived, so that is what you want to dig into. This is why just looking at a list of activities is not enough. You must go deeper.

As an example, consider a "self-service" platform. On one hand, it could be implemented to dramatically improve operations. On the other hand, it could provide minimal value. Often "self-service" means that a central group of people no longer provides the service, which can be great. Now you can go to a website and help yourself. But even though it eliminated the need for that central group, it might not deliver net value to the overall organization—not if the collective cost of all those individuals now serving themselves outweighs the original cost of the central group. The work has just been pushed to different people.

The assessment of business value achievement is a tricky thing to wade through, but it is the most important question of them all. However, there is no point expending the energy for this if the first three parts of your Search uncovered material issues. Most troubled Transformation Programs will never make it to part 4—they will end up in Rescue mode well before reaching it. Speaking of Rescue, it's time to head over and look at those options.

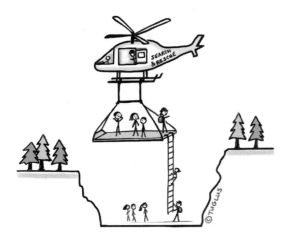

Rescue: Can It Be Rescued?

The assessment is complete. You know with confidence and clarity where your Transformation Program stands. Suppose your suspicions have been confirmed. You have concluded that it is, in fact, not on the path to achieving your business goals. Now what? What do you do? Can it be rescued? Without being there with you, I can't answer that, but what I can do is give you the rundown of your options.

But before I do that, let's be honest about what is going through your head. If you are the CEO or the division head who sponsored the transformation, then right now you are furiously thinking through the potential impacts on the business plan and possible political ramifications: *What position could this put me in personally? What will I tell the board, how do I explain it? Things may need to be written off. Can we still salvage something and amortize it? How much will this impact the business plan forecasts that have been communicated externally? And we have to consider the press. Did we make any public announcements about this transformation?*

Is there reputational risk? And the employees. How will they feel? How much do they already know? And how badly did we need this transformation to succeed? Do we have time to try again?

Your head is spinning. Give yourself a day to absorb it all, to work through those thoughts. Then start thinking about your Rescue plans and draft the first version. Thinking through your options and getting them documented will help you think more clearly about communications and politics. And, of course, it will also help you decide what to do.

CONSIDER YOUR OPTIONS

As you assess a transformation, it is important not to get caught in a "keep versus cancel" paradigm. The ultimate answer is often multifaceted. Perhaps this particular endeavor is failing as is, but the business value must be achieved. There may be salvageable components, even if it needs an entirely new Transformation Program, one supplied with better Preparation and real Recon. Your solution will involve at least one, but more likely a combination, of the following actions:

Coach: You can hire a coach for your transformation leader. In most scenarios, this is a high-leverage move, yielding significant benefit for the cost. In a best-case scenario, things are pretty good. The program took a few wrong turns, and the greatest need is to get that transformation leader some high-caliber coaching. Maybe the leader wasn't ready for the role. Or maybe you want to give them another chance before making a final call. Find an experienced transformation executive to serve as a coach.

Advise: You and/or your executive team members would benefit from an outside advisor. Perhaps the resistance to transformation across the executive team was higher than you expected. And those resisters (who look suspiciously like dragons) are impeding progress, intentionally or unintentionally. If so, that is something for you to personally work on. In this case, try to hire an expert advisor who can spend time with you, or the entire executive team, or—even better—both. In the less favorable scenarios, where you are halting the program, an expert advisor will provide especially valuable guidance if you are planning to relaunch the program.

Add: There are gaps in the team. One common gap is not investing in enough real transformation program management expertise. Another popular discovery is that some business areas did not commit enough expert talent. It is also quite common to find that teams have underestimated the sheer volume of tracking and organizing required, and lack enough support roles. Supplement gaps in the team accordingly.

Replace: Your transformation leader just isn't cutting it. Maybe you took a chance on someone lacking transformation experience. Or you have overwhelmed someone with a role that is more complex than they were ready for. Or you just hired the wrong person for the job. Replace them. Review the traits of a great transformation leader as you hire (see page 78). The new leader will assess the rest of the team. Their first step will be an in-depth, comprehensive assessment. Be prepared for changes. They may need entirely new program management talent. They may also need to replace other core team members, especially if the program was not staffed with top talent.

Replan: The program is not on a trajectory to achieve meaningful business value in a reasonable time period. It is time to freeze and replan. It is possible to have a good team but need to replan—unexpected challenges appear during all transformation journeys. But often you also need to replace at least part of the Transformation team. Especially if this is not the first replanning of this program.

Reposition: Something has occurred that is causing a material change in business needs. Probably that annoying world that never sits still. Part (or all) of the transformation is no longer relevant. It is time to freeze all or part of the initiative, and run a Recon-like activity to reset your transformation's goals and roadmap. Alternatively, the need is that the program must be massively accelerated to achieve value faster. In this case, run a Recon-like activity concurrent to the program, then switch over to the new plan.

Redefine: The program goals were poorly defined. What was missed? Was a Recon effort not conducted to get the necessary mid-level definition and roadmap? If so, freeze the program and execute a Recon Mission. Or does the issue go beyond that? Is the high-level vision suspect? Freeze the initiative, and conduct an assessment of disruption, competition, and current state. Do you *have* to freeze? You may have reasons to keep the program going, even in the face of this. In which case, conduct the assessment in parallel. Then head to Salvage to determine what program work can be applied to the new vision and direction.

Salvage: Things are really bad. You may need to start over. The program isn't delivering, or it is delivering business value that is not worth the continued investment. Freeze and run an assessment to determine what is salvageable. Remove the leader, and bring in experts to perform the assessment.

Surrender: Game over. You're done and you're not doing it again. You do not believe the organization needs the intended business value, or that it is worth the journey. (Or you just do not have enough energy to even consider it.) Kill it. The dragons celebrate.

Cleanup: Manage the downstream impacts of ending this or revising the goals. Adjust the business forecast for expected benefits that will no longer materialize, like revenue or customer acquisition. Write off any capital investments as necessary. Address any impacts on other programs that were depending upon this.

Start over: You can't salvage this particular Transformation Program and team. But even though it was a disaster, the business case is still strong. You need this. You know what to do. Clear the slate. Start at the beginning. Go back to phase 1 (see page 15), and do it right this time.

HERE BE DRAGONS

A Final Note

What are you going to do about it? Did your program just need a little help? Or was it truly troubled? Business transformation is fraught with peril. The magnitude of know-how and commitment are often underestimated. Statistically speaking, you will face troubled transformations in your career, and you will need to investigate.

Strike fast, because the world is still moving forward. Assess the damage, then get up, dust yourself off, and figure out where to go from here. No matter how painful it is, you need to focus on business value. What is essential for your organization to survive and thrive? The way out of a failing Transformation Program has a striking parallel to the way into a successful one. You'll need to figure out where you really stand (current state), what's changed in the world (disruption), what is truly important to achieve (vision), how to make it possible (recon), and go forward from there . . . . Sound familiar? Good. Then nothing, not even fear of the unknown, is standing in your way.

Quick Guides

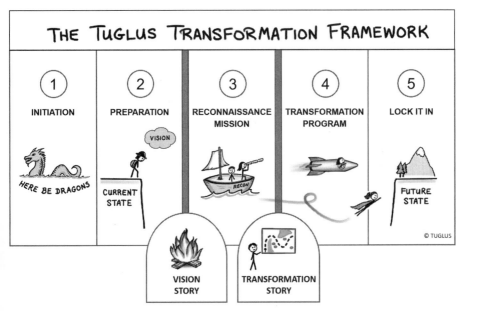

JOURNEY AT A GLANCE

Initiation
(1) Immerse yourself in the laws of the land with the foundational Tuglus Transformation Laws.

Preparation
(2) Formulate a compelling, value-driven vision. Assess Disruption and Current State. Deftly circumnavigate four pitfalls. Gather the information necessary to build your Vision Story.

Vision Story
(○) Build belief in the need to change as you confidently share your vision for the future and why transformation is vital.

Reconnaissance
(3) Conduct a Recon Mission to explore the future state and how to get there. Produce a mid-level definition of the future state and draft a roadmap for achieving it. Leap over more pitfalls. Estimate resources, budget, and time. Activate your superpower.

Transformation Story
(○) Combine Recon outputs with the Vision Story to make your vision real to people. Share what the future looks like and how your organization will get there. Use this story to gain commitment to transform.

Transformation Program
(4) Pick up some pro tips for setting up and running your Transformation Program. Build rocket ships and fly over more pitfalls as you construct your future state.

Lock It In
(5) Lock in the business value of your transformation to ensure your organization takes advantage of all the new potential you have created. Catapult over two final pitfalls.

SECRET PITFALLS MAP

② PREPARATION

The Allure of Benchmarking
Just Technology, Please
Technology as a Magic Process Fix
Centralize It All

③ RECONNAISSANCE

Too Deep, Too Soon
Outsourcing Ownership

Cutting Business Value
One Process Fits All

TRANSFORMATION ④

Unrealized Potential
Abrupt Handoff

LOCK IT IN ⑤

Acknowledgments

FIRST, I WANT to thank all the people who, upon hearing I was writing a book, immediately believed it would come to fruition and be great. There is not enough room here to mention you all, but know that I appreciated your confidence.

Second, I want to thank all the fearless people who said, "Yes, of course," when I asked you to review an early draft, knowing that I'd never written a book before. Your thoughtful feedback was instrumental in helping me make this book easy-to-consume and—critically—not boring. Thank you for joining me in my quest to help people understand what it really takes to lead a business transformation. I greatly appreciate all the time you spent and the conversations we had. So thank you John Boris, Pamela Burt, Val Gui, Pat Hillberg, Marcy Klevorn, Lesley Ma, Tim McCabe, Debi Parizek, Pat Quint, Ben Sabloff, Lee Senderov, and Tom Tang. And a special shout-out to Patrick Barrow, secret weapon extraordinaire. You have all helped make this book what it is.

About the Author

ANGIE TUGLUS is an expert in business transformation. She enjoys making complex organizational initiatives possible, from operational redesign, business pivots, and culture change to new business creation.

She credits some of her success in transformation to her love of learning how things work—industries, companies, technologies, household appliances.... Upon occasion, she has been known to follow someone she's just met back to their office for a tour to learn about their business (but not in a creepy kind of way).

She began her career in technology start-ups and later applied her passion for transformation in large corporations undergoing major change, including Ford Motor Company, GMAC, and Ally Financial. She has held executive roles including COO, CIO, and EVP of Product & Project Delivery. She holds a BS in materials engineering from Northwestern University, an MBA from Duke University's Fuqua School of Business, and an Executive Scholar Certificate from Northwestern University's Kellogg School of Management.

Tuglus now serves as a strategic advisor to executives in companies undergoing transformation or extreme growth. Her diverse clients, who range from start-ups to large corporations, all have one thing in common: they are serious about transformation. Learn more about how to make transformation possible at www.tuglus.com.